THE LIGHT
Is On
FOR YOU

THE LIFE-CHANGING POWER
OF CONFESSION

CARDINAL DONALD WUERL
ARCHBISHOP OF WASHINGTON

the WORD
among us®
press

Published by The Word Among Us Press
7115 Guilford Drive, Suite 100
Frederick, Maryland 21704
www.wau.org

18 17 16 15 14   1 2 3 4 5

ISBN: 978-1-59325-250-2
eISBN: 978-1-59325-454-4

Cover design by John Hamilton Designs
Cover photo by Andrea Kelley of
St. Mary's Catholic Church, Lincoln, Nebraska

Made and printed in the United States of America

Library of Congress Control Number: 2013956587

THE LIGHT
Is On
FOR YOU

THE LIFE-CHANGING POWER
OF CONFESSION

CONTENTS

FOREWORD

By Scott Hahn

Confession is nothing new. As long as sin has been in the world, so have confession, penance, and reconciliation. Indeed, God delivered history's original invitation to confession just moments after mankind's original sin.

Read the opening pages of the Bible. Adam and Eve fall to temptation and eat the forbidden fruit. Immediately, God asks Adam, "Where are you?" (Genesis 3:9).

Now, did you ever wonder about the strangeness of that question? God is all-knowing and all-seeing. He knows Adam's whereabouts without asking.

Yet ask he does. And when Adam answers evasively, God follows with two more questions: "Who told you that you were naked? Have you eaten of the tree of which I commanded you not to eat?" (Genesis 3:11). And when Adam continues to avoid the self-incriminating truth, God asks Eve, "What is this that you have done?" (3:13).

God isn't looking to be informed. He already knows the score. So, in asking questions, he must want something else from Adam and Eve.

He wants confession. He wants the primal couple to confess their sin with true sorrow.

Later in the Book of Genesis, we find the same pattern. Cain murders his brother, Abel, and God asks, "Where is Abel your brother?" Cain doesn't answer the question, but still, God does not accuse him. Instead, he invites him to confess, and even presents him with evidence of his crime: "What have you done? The voice of your brother's blood is crying to me from the ground" (Genesis 4:10).

We see, in the stories of Adam and Eve and Cain, that men and women don't take hints, especially when it means admitting their own faults. We'd rather blame others, blame our heredity or environment, or even blame God. But we're not likely to rush forward to blame ourselves.

So when God gave his law to Moses, he established confession as a cornerstone, and this time he gave clear instructions. Take, for example, Leviticus 5:5-6, which deals with the various sins people commit when they swear rashly: "When a man is guilty in any of these, he shall confess the sin he has committed, and he shall bring his guilt offering to the LORD for the sin which he has committed, a female from the flock, a lamb or a goat, for a sin offering; and the priest shall make atonement for him for his sin."

By giving his people a clear plan of action, God made it possible for individuals to confess their sins. First, he explicitly insisted upon such a confession. Then, he gave the sinners something to do—a liturgical act of sacrifice and penance. And finally, he insisted that they do all this with the help and the intercession of a priest. All of these elements would survive intact throughout the history of Israel and of the renewed Israel, the Church of Jesus Christ.

The old covenant was never abolished but rather was fulfilled and transformed with the new covenant of Jesus Christ.

In their ancient form, the old covenant sacrifices were never enough, and they always pointed to something greater than themselves. God had established them to foreshadow their future fulfillment. In one way, these sacrifices were a hint of the greatness to come, but in another way, they were clearly inadequate: "But in these sacrifices there is a reminder of sin year after year. For it is impossible that the blood of bulls and goats should take away sins" (Hebrews 10:3-4).

Even with the sacrifices, the chosen people fell into sin again and again, and no offering could make up for their offenses against an infinitely perfect God. The high priest in Jerusalem stood every day "offering repeatedly the same sacrifices, which can never take away sins" (Hebrews 10:11).

The old ways would not do. If sacred rituals were to take away sins, then God himself would have to serve as high priest. And so he did.

Moreover, Jesus had the authority to share his high priestly power of forgiveness with his chosen apostles, and that's precisely what he did on the day of his resurrection: "He breathed on them, and said to them, 'Receive the Holy Spirit. If you forgive the sins of any, they are forgiven; if you retain the sins of any, they are retained'" (John 20:22-23).

The apostles exercised this authority and preached confession to the first Christians. "If we confess our sins, [God] is faithful and just," said St. John, "and will forgive our sins and cleanse us from all unrighteousness" (1 John 1:9). St. Paul makes the further clarification that "confession" is something you do "with your mouth," not just with your heart and mind (cf. Romans 10:10).

St. James, for his part, took up the matter of confession at the end of his discussion of the sacramental duties of the clergy. The term he used for clergymen is the Greek *presbuterous*, which literally means "elders," but which is the root of the English word "priest." Here's what James said:

> Is any among you sick? Let him call for the elders [*presbuterous*] of the church, and let them pray over him, anointing him with oil in the name of the Lord; and the prayer of faith will save the sick man, and the Lord will raise him up; and if he has committed sins, he will be forgiven. Therefore confess your sins to one another, and pray for one another, that you may be healed. (James 5:14-16)

Whenever you see the word "therefore" in Scripture, you have to ask yourself what it's there for. In this passage, James is clearly setting the practice of confession in connection with the priest's healing ministry. Because priests are healers, we call upon them to anoint our bodies when we are ill, and *therefore*, even more eagerly do we go to them for the healing sacrament of forgiveness when our souls are sick with sin.

Note that St. James does not exhort his congregation to confess their sins to Jesus alone, nor does he tell them to confess their sins silently, in their hearts. They may do all these things, all to their credit, but they will not yet be faithful to the word of God preached by St. James—not until they confess their sins aloud to "another," specifically to a *presbyter*, a priest.

Is It Healthy?

After all that testimony, the modern-day objections to Confession seem almost absurd. "Yes," we can hear the skeptics say, "but is it healthy? Is it healthy to think about sin and guilt and all that?"

We could just as easily counter: what are the alternatives? Counseling, medications, therapies, diversions—these all have their place. But none of them can heal the deepest wounds caused by sin. Our hearts are restless and will remain restless until they receive the divinely prescribed cure.

Still, I would go further than that. I'd say that Confession is the healthiest thing going. Confession does for our souls what doctors, dietitians, physical therapists, and pharmacists do for our bodies.

Think about all that we do to keep our bodies in working order. We go for regular checkups. And no one has to remind us to brush our teeth, take a shower, and pop the pills for whatever ails us. All this is good for us, and it's good for everyone around us too. No one wants to work beside us if we decide to stop showering.

Well, if we spend so much effort on the care of our bodies, shouldn't we be spending more time on our souls? After all, our bodies will pass away soon enough, but our souls will live on forever.

What's more, our decisions about our spiritual health and hygiene will have a tremendous effect on the people around us. Nothing serves family life and workplace dynamics as well as a clean soul and the advice of a good confessor.

On the other hand, nothing hurts our relationships and our mental health more than the burden of sin and guilt. Confession is free health care—comprehensive coverage for every family, from cradle to grave. Christ is the divine Physician, and unlike human physicians, he can guarantee us a cure every time.

In fact, he can guarantee us immortality. Any doctor who could do all that would have long lines outside his office door.

I pray that this wonderful book is read by many, many Catholics. When my prayer is answered, I look forward to finding long lines at the confessionals!

Confession, as I said, is nothing new. Sin is nothing new. What is new with this book is the fresh approach of one of the great teachers of our generation. Cardinal Donald Wuerl is—like the great Fathers of the early Church, Cyril, Chrysostom, Ambrose, Augustine—a theologian of the first rank, but a bishop above all.

Scott Hahn is author of many books, including Lord, Have Mercy: The Healing Power of Confession. *He holds the Father Michael Scanlan Chair in Biblical Theology and the New Evangelization at Franciscan University of Steubenville. He is founder of the St. Paul Center for Biblical Theology.*

LEAVING THE LIGHT ON

One of the great benefits that comes with the work of being an archbishop is that I'm able to attend youth events—many decades after I've passed what can reasonably be called my "youth." I get an invitation to World Youth Day, wherever it may be celebrated that year. I help to host the annual Youth Rally for Life in Washington, D.C. I've addressed the Vigil for Life at the Basilica Shrine of the Immaculate Conception. And in my regular rounds, I visit many high schools and college campus ministry programs in Washington and Maryland.

I enjoy the best view of each event because I'm usually speaking, and so I can look out at a crowd—often standing room only—of eager, engaged faces. They're smiling even though they've made sacrifices. At the vigil, many of them have stayed up all night in prayer. At the rally, many have traveled long hours on a bus and then have stood in long lines, sometimes even in the cold rain. Yet these young people are smiling, because they're happy to be Catholic and they're happy about what makes them Catholic. They love the things that are *distinctive* about our faith. They love the Mass, of course, and they love our traditions of prayer. They love to be with Jesus in Eucharistic adoration. They love the Rosary. They love the Church's enduring commitment to the pro-life cause and to true social justice.

What never fails to bring joy to my heart, however, is their love for the Sacrament of Penance.

Call it "Reconciliation," "Confession," or any of the titles found in the *Catechism of the Catholic Church*—these young people make the most of it. At youth events, the lines are long, and the organizers keep them going even as the speakers say their piece. From the podium I can watch the lines moving along. As young men and women take their turn at the confessional, others arrive at the end of the line to take their place. When there are many priests hearing confessions, the lines stretch like rivers through the venue. In a place as large as the Verizon Center, that makes for a mighty river.

Young Catholics have taken to this sacrament in a way that, it pains me to say, an older generation sometimes finds difficult to understand. Perhaps in the 1960s or 1970s, they thought Confession was a thing of the past. Some of them rued its decline but grumbled that the decline was inevitable. Others welcomed its decline because they misunderstood the sacrament or had once had a bad experience of it.

When a newspaper prematurely published Mark Twain's obituary, the author quipped, "The reports of my death have been greatly exaggerated." The Church today is saying quite clearly that the reports of Confession's demise are simply wrong. The Church is saying this through its youth, who stand in long lines for the sacrament when they are given the opportunity.

The Church is saying this, moreover, through current events. As I work on this book on Confession, it is early in the ministry of Pope Francis, whom journalists have already named "the Pope of Mercy." How did he earn that title? He never tires of inviting us all to go frequently to the sacrament of mercy. And people are responding: recent headlines report studies saying that there was a spike in the demand for Confession, for example, among Catholics in the United Kingdom in the months after Pope Francis's election.

When people are given the opportunity for Confession, they usually take it. And when some people seize the chance, others eagerly follow. A friend of mine recently found himself trapped at an airport gate when his flight was delayed. He noticed that one of his fellow passengers was a priest—the Roman collar gave him away—so he figured he'd make the best of a frustrating situation. My friend asked the priest if he would hear his confession, and Father was happy to oblige. They stepped off to an empty gate nearby, where they would have privacy. As my friend made his confession, a curious thing happened: a line formed! Catholics in the crowd saw that a priest was available. They had time on their hands. They took advantage of the opportunity.

In 2008, when Pope Benedict XVI visited the United States and celebrated Mass for fifty thousand people at Nationals Park in Washington, D.C., we made provisions for the many people who came to take advantage of Confession. We reserved a restricted area at the park. The lines were long. I am told that someone from the television team covering the event left the broadcast booth and went down to the confession area, where he was told he could not enter because it was private and not for media coverage. It took him two more attempts to get into the confession area before he could convince someone that he was there not to do a story on the confessions but to go to Confession himself! He wanted to go because he had been so moved by what he saw happening that morning.

Confession serves a real human need that has not diminished with the passage of time. The human race has, unfortunately, not outgrown its tendency to sin. People sin. You do and I do. Everyone does, and when we do, we feel the burden of our transgressions. Jesus Christ came to give us rest from such burdens, and he gave his Church the power and the means to unburden us. He did this when he instituted his sacrament of forgiveness.

And so we go. If we see our chance in an airport, or at an arena, or across a field at World Youth Day, we make our way, we stand in line, we confess our sins, and we receive God's forgiveness—something that cannot be bought, cannot be replaced, and cannot be outdone.

Confession is not a thing of the past. It has, right now, all the vigor of youth.

Observations and anecdotes, I recognize, hardly add up to a trend. The youth events I attend are *special* events, and the young people who flock to Confession at a rally may not respond so readily back home. I know, moreover, that rallies and vigils tend to attract those who are already committed to the faith.

It is also true that what I see at youth rallies is not what a typical priest sees in his parish on a Saturday afternoon.

Indeed, it's been many years since ordinary parishes—both in the United States and in Europe—have experienced long lines at the confessional on a non-Lenten Saturday.

According to recent research, three-quarters of Catholics report that they *never* participate in the sacrament or that they do so less than once a year. The numbers are better for practicing Catholics—those who attend Mass every Sunday—but the bottom line is still disappointing: slightly more than 60 percent of *practicing* Catholics go to Confession once a year or more. Once a year is the minimum the Church asks Catholics to go to Confession to fulfill their "Easter duty." So a slight majority of the minority of Catholics who regularly attend Mass are putting in their minimal effort.

Once a year is not very often, and yet even that seems too much for many Catholics. Yet far less than a century ago, it was considered *normal* for those who received Communion on Sunday to have confessed their sins on Saturday. That is a living memory for some of the oldest members of our parishes.

Confession satisfies a normal human need in our fallen world. It lavishly benefits the one who confesses. It requires little time, and it costs nothing. Yet the few who receive it do so only rarely.

Promoting the sacrament should be like selling water to the thirsty, but it's not. It's more like offering ice cubes in the Arctic Circle.

Why?

Since I am shepherd of a large diocese, the question is of more than academic interest to me. God has called me to the care of the multitude of souls who live and work in the capital city of the United States of America. God will hold me accountable for all I have done and all I have failed to do in the interest of their salvation.

Thus, the situation worries me, as it preoccupies many pastors, many bishops, and the pope himself. In our archdiocese, we recognized the status quo as an urgent problem, and we set ourselves to solving it—or at least coming up with the beginning of a solution.

Part of the problem, we concluded, is a lack of knowledge. Many Catholics simply do not know what Confession is or even what a sacrament is. Many received their religious training during a time of great confusion in the Church, when it was unfashionable to speak of doctrine or facts. Teachers were encouraged, instead, to communicate an *experience* of God's love, but to do so without reference to the Creed, the sacraments, or Catholic tradition. It didn't work very well.

Laypeople who knew little about Catholic doctrine were unable to withstand the tsunami of secularism that has become so common in our culture since the last decades of the twentieth century. Confession has no place in a worldview that sees moral truths as relative and that leaves it up to the individual to decide what is right or wrong. More than one recent pope has observed that the greatest loss of our time is the loss of a sense of sin.

In the Archdiocese of Washington, as was the case in my earlier pastoral assignment in Pittsburgh, we agreed that the communication of clear doctrine would be an important component of our efforts to promote Confession. Doctrine by itself, however, would never be enough. As Pope Francis tells us so often, we need to "go out" to others.

Like those priests at the vigils and the rallies—and like that lone priest at the airport gate—we would have to provide *opportunities* for Confession. We would also have to make those opportunities known. We would have to send out an invitation. We would probably have to repeat the invitation many times. We would have to make a strong effort to welcome our people home to Confession.

The key would be to welcome them *home*.

What emerged was a program with the theme "The Light Is ON for You." It was launched during Lent, the forty-day penitential season before Easter, because that is a time traditionally associated with Confession and conversion of heart. For the older generations—many of whose members have been away from the sacrament—the invitation would evoke memories of the piety of their childhood years.

We chose our theme because we wanted to suggest a homecoming. "Leaving the light on" is what family members do for one another. I grew up in a hilltop city neighborhood, whose narrow streets were lined with the homes of hardworking families. If Dad or Mom were pulling the night shift, the porch light stayed on till they arrived home. Nurses, police officers, and railroad employees regularly tiptoed in before dawn. If your teenaged siblings went to a ball game across town, the light stayed on until they returned, no matter how late the game ran with extra innings or overtime. "Leaving the light on" is basic family courtesy. The light is a beacon of love, care, concern, and safety—the good things we associate with home.

But we had another good reason for choosing our theme. The electric light on the confessional is the customary sign that a penitent may enter.

The program would gradually unfold over several years. Our goal was simple: we wanted to extend a simple invitation to people to go to Confession—to let them know that it was available and convenient—and to assure them that they would be lovingly and generously received into their spiritual home.

The goal was simple, but achieving it would require effort. How could we reach all the people we wanted to touch? Active Catholics could be reached through homilies, parish bulletins, the archdiocesan newspaper, the archbishop's pastoral letters, and posters in the church vestibule. All those means are good, and active Catholics did (and do) need to take greater advantage of the sacrament. But what about those who are estranged from the Church? What about those who are even estranged from their Catholic family members? What about those who rarely go near a Catholic church?

We wanted our message to reach all of them, every one. So the program called for widespread advertising using radio, social media, podcasts, metro and bus ads, and roadside billboards. The message was constant and clear: "The Light Is ON for You."

In every Catholic church across the archdiocese, every Wednesday night during Lent from 6:30 to 8:00 p.m., the light would be on so that people would know that a priest (or more than one priest) was inside, waiting for them.

We made sure that each parish provided ample time to hear confessions. So we set the baseline at an hour and a half, although many priests stayed longer when there were lines or when a penitent showed up at the last minute.

We made sure that the time was convenient to many people's work schedules. One time slot, of course, cannot accommodate everyone, so we also invited people to make an appointment or take advantage of regularly scheduled parish confessions.

Another benefit was the fact that the light was on in *every* Catholic parish. Some people feel uneasy about confessing to priests who know them, so they won't go in their home parish—and avoid the sacrament altogether. Knowing that a priest was available on their route home from work, many people seized their moment of assured anonymity.

On site and online, we provided instructional literature for those who had been away so long that they had forgotten the practicalities of Confession. For example, the Act of Contrition was printed and made readily available on church property everywhere.

The program succeeded as we had hoped. Catholics came home—because they saw that the light was on and they knew that the door was open.

For me, one of the early indications that the program was a success was a note I received from a friend who had been visiting Washington for business. While trying to get through town for an appointment, he got stuck behind a bus in D.C.

rush-hour traffic. That fact alone could generate sufficient cause for repentance and confession. But the bus had an advertisement for "The Light Is ON for You." As the vehicles in his lane inched forward, my friend could not help but contemplate the message. He was so intrigued that as soon as he got home, he went online to learn more about it. Last year, the diocese where he lives initiated a similar program. In fact, many other dioceses throughout the United States and even Canada have launched their own efforts to renew the Sacrament of Reconciliation, based on all that we have learned.

Comments made to me by two priests, one recently ordained and the other, a pastor for decades, highlight the joy and success of this effort to renew the Sacrament of Confession. The younger priest recounted his experience the first time the program was introduced. He told me that on the first Wednesday evening, he heard confessions for about forty-five minutes. The following week it took about an hour and a half. By the time we were into the fourth week, he said that confessions went on until nearly 9:00 p.m. That night, he returned to his room filled with emotion. As he sat and reflected, he thought, "This is why I became a priest."

The older priest stopped me at an event and said, "Archbishop, I heard a confession last Wednesday evening. That confession alone was worth this whole program. Please keep it up." That minimal comment speaks volumes, as priests are naturally reticent to speak at all about their experience of hearing a confession.

Begun in 2007, the program is still going strong. In fact, it's become an integral part of the local Church's life—and as a result, Confession has become an important part of the lives of many Catholics.

By necessity, I have had to live much of my adult life at a distance from my family. Though I was raised in western Pennsylvania, my pastoral assignments, since I was in my twenties, have taken me to places as far-flung as Rome, Italy, and Seattle, Washington. Believe me, I know the joy of homecoming in the natural order of life. So much more do I treasure every homecoming in the supernatural order—the sacramental way that Jesus established because he loves us.

Pope Francis has not tired of pointing out that we are a Church of sinners. In his first extended interview with the press, he identified himself as "a sinner" first of all. This should arrive as news to no one who understands the Christian faith. Yet it made headlines in all the news media. The Catholic message is indeed news. The gospel of mercy is good news in a world that is often full of bad tidings.

It is good news to me. Like Pope Francis, I have to admit that I am a sinner, and I am grateful that I can make that admission in the Sacrament of Reconciliation. *Regular* confession makes for a happier life. That is the promise of Jesus. It is the experience of the saints. It is the message of the Church. It is the subject of this book, which I hope can be a practical guide, with stories to make the Church's principles clear and more memorable, including personal stories of everyday Catholics in the "From the Pews" section at the end of each chapter.

Confession has been my habitual homecoming since I was a child. It is a consolation and a joy, and such joy, our faith teaches us, is meant for everyone. It is our vocation to bring it to as many people as possible.

Mercy will always be news. It is always something fresh from God, and it will never get old. When we envisioned the theme for the Lenten Confession program, I was pleased with its creativity. Then I happened upon a text that shows the same idea expressed a very long time ago on the other side of the world. In the early years of Christianity, a North African convert named Tertullian observed that Baptism and Penance are "the two lighthouses of salvation."[1] Lighthouses are the great lamps that lead ships to safe harbor. After a long voyage, they are the sign for weary sailors that they have arrived home. A lighthouse is a familiar sight, and yet it always arrives as news—as good news.

Another Father of the early Church, the great St. Jerome, called Baptism and Confession the "two doors" by which Catholics enter their true home.[2]

The Church is indeed the family of God. That is, perhaps, one of the most pervasive messages of the *Catechism of the Catholic Church* (see, for example, 1, 542, 759, 815, 854, 959, 1632, 1655, 2233). As Catholics, we belong to God's household (Ephesians 2:19; 1 Timothy 3:15; 1 Peter 4:17). We'll be restless until we follow the light that Tertullian saw in the second century and walk through the door that St. Jerome opened for his own parishioners in the fourth century. We'll be restless until we're at home where we belong.

The confessional door is open for us. The light is on.

From the Pews

It had been much too long. And as the months passed by, I felt more and more guilt and embarrassment. What would the priest say? How could I explain my absence or even review my actions and sins after such a long period of time? Almost every Saturday, for months on end, these kinds of questions went through my mind.

One day, on a pilgrimage to a shrine in New York City, the gentle promptings of God's Holy Spirit that I had been resisting on all of those Saturdays became even stronger and more insistent. I took some time to pray in the chapel while a parade of people marched by me on their way to Confession. The time had arrived to join them.

After reading some psalms, I decided on a face-to-face celebration so that I could get the most help possible with my situation. Then I took my place in line and, after waiting for some time, finally entered the confessional. Just as I had finished saying how long it had been, and before I even had time to say another word, Father interrupted me. With a big grin on his face, he said, "Welcome back! I'm so glad you came!" I was almost speechless. Here was Jesus with all the unconditional love that I had needed for so long but had been too afraid to seek. Alleluia! I was home in some brand new, indescribable way.

CHAPTER ONE

WHY GO TO CONFESSION?

Confession has always been the favorite sacrament of novelists and filmmakers. Even non-Catholic artists recognize the power of the confessional. In fact, sometimes non-Catholics, from a distance, see the truth that we Catholics too often miss.

There is a telling scene in *The Marble Faun* by the American novelist Nathaniel Hawthorne. Hilda, the novel's troubled heroine, surveys the long line of confessional booths in a church in Rome.

> Approaching one of the confessionals, she saw a woman kneeling within. Just as Hilda drew near, the penitent rose. . . . Hilda was so struck with the peace and joy in the woman's face, that, as the latter retired, she could not help speaking to her. "You look very happy!" said she. "Is it so sweet, then, to go to the confessional?"
>
> "O, very sweet, my dear *signorina*!" answered the woman, with moistened eyes and an affectionate smile; for she was so thoroughly softened with what she had been doing, that she felt as if Hilda were her younger sister. "My heart is at rest now."[3]

Hilda is not Catholic. She shares with the author, Hawthorne, a New England Puritan background. Yet she has no need to ask the penitent why anyone would go to Confession.

In fact, Hilda immediately enters a nearby confessional in search of the kind of peace she has observed in the face of the penitent.

The British author Charlotte Bronte presents a very similar scene in her novel *Villette*. The narrator, Lucy, an English Protestant living in Belgium, says she is "perishing for a word of advice or an accent of comfort." She recalls, "I had been living for some weeks quite alone. I had been ill; I had a pressure of affliction on my mind of which it would hardly any longer endure the weight."[4] Again, like Hawthorne's Hilda, she expects that she can find relief and consolation in the confessional booth of a Catholic church.

These authors (and their characters) did not need to be Catholic to recognize the good reasons to go to Confession. Unfortunately, as the characters find out in the course of the narrative, only Catholics can receive the sacrament (except in extraordinary circumstances).

In their naiveté, both Hilda and Lucy make a strong case for the natural advantages of Confession. The sacrament is a safe place where people can break their unbearable silence and lay down their heavy burdens. It is a place where we can speak in certain trust and receive good counsel.

Both novelists, Hawthorne and Bronte, had native anti-Catholic prejudices, and yet they perceived the natural value of confessing one's sins. Confession, they recognized, had the power to move a plot forward—to add new dimensions to a narrative and make it higher, deeper, broader, and fuller. In art as in life, Confession can bring an anxious drama to a satisfactory resolution.

What is true of Confession in the natural order—and even in literary fiction!—is infinitely truer of Confession in the supernatural order.

There are many good reasons to go to Confession—we could fill a book with them. But the best reason is this one: it satisfies a genuine and profound human need. We need to confess because we have sinned, and sin brings about a decisive rupture in our relationship with God. God is merciful and always ready to forgive us, but he will not compel us to love or to be reconciled. God created us to be free—and he respects our freedom.

Our need for Confession is as old as our species. Biblical religion begins, in the Book of Genesis, with the story of God's creation of man and woman. God created Adam and Eve and pronounced them to be "very good" (Genesis 1:31). He placed them in a lush garden and said, "You may eat freely of every tree of the garden; but of the tree of the knowledge of good and evil you shall not eat, for in the day that you eat of it you shall die" (Genesis 2:16-17). The tempter, however, said to them, "You will not die. For God knows that when you eat of it your eyes will be opened, and you will be like God, knowing good and evil" (3:4-5).

Free to choose between the word of God and the word of the tempter, Adam and Eve choose unwisely. They eat the forbidden fruit. They choose their own desires over God's will and plan.

The *Catechism* explains that this biblical account uses figurative language to convey the truth of a historical event. Sin entered the world through the decision of a human being to choose self over God. God is not responsible for the evil in the world.

God, in fact, gives Adam every opportunity to admit that he has sinned and to repent. The Almighty asks a series of questions, the answers to which he already knows. But Adam adamantly refuses to confess and take responsibility for his sin. Instead, he conceals his own guilt and blames his wife.

Adam and Eve soon become aware of the effects of their sin and are filled with shame before God—hiding from him rather than seeking his face. This was not the way it was meant to be. Once sin entered into life and into our world, harmony with God was shattered, and the human family's whole network of relationships with each other and the world began to unravel. The pattern repeats itself, in general outline, in the Genesis account of Cain's murder of Abel. Cain commits a horrible sin; he is confronted; he refuses to confess and repent.

The sins of one generation cascade into the next, leading to the flood in Noah's time, the confusion of languages at the Tower of Babel, the destruction of Sodom in the time of Abraham, the enslavement of Israel in Egypt, and the Babylonian exile. All these later catastrophes trace their genealogy to that first sinful action—the fundamental breakdown that we call original sin. It is the fault line at the center of the fallen human condition.

Each one of us is an heir to Adam and Eve. We are members of the human family. We trace our lineage back to that couple and their failure to respect God's plan. They freely chose to take actions that shattered the harmony that God had created, not only for themselves, but also for us. Their sin is reflected in us and mirrored in our daily lives. This helps to explain why it is so difficult to do the good, to do what we know we should do.

Yet we are not lost; we are not left to our own devices. St. Paul, writing to the Corinthians, says that just as in Adam sin entered the world—with death and all its consequences—so too grace and new creation come to us in Jesus Christ. Just as death came through a human being, so too the resurrection of the dead came through a human being. As in Adam all people die, so in Christ all may be brought to life—a fullness of life, a new creation already beginning in us through grace (see 1 Corinthians 15).

Within us, the new life—the life of Christ—struggles with the old, the heritage of Adam. The "old" is concerned only with the self. The new person, baptized and alive in God's grace, is directed to God, Christ, and our neighbors. This struggle, deep within our human nature, has continued from the time of Adam and Eve's sin. Our baptism washes away original sin, but its effects still remain.

It is Jesus Christ who leads us back to God the Father. Jesus overcomes the tragic alienation of sin and restores harmony to creation. Jesus restores our relationship with God, which will lead to full communion in glory. It is for this reason that we identify Christ as the "new Adam." In Jesus, humanity gets another chance, a new start. Grace is the beginning of a new creation for all those baptized into Christ.

❖ ❖ ❖ ❖ ❖

Even now, however, many years after our redemption by Christ, we still must struggle. God leaves us free, and we must choose to correspond to divine grace.

St. Paul was a man of great personal discipline and intelligence. He had dedicated his entire life to God from an early age, and yet he still found himself falling into habits of sin:

> I do not understand my own actions. For I do not do what I want, but I do the very thing I hate. . . . I can will what is right, but I cannot do it. For I do not do the good I want, but the evil I do not want is what I do. Now if I do what I do not want, it is no longer I that do it, but sin which dwells within me. (Romans 7:15, 18-20)

St. Paul's cry from the heart is something each of us has experienced. Why is it that we have the best of intentions, sincerely making New Year's resolutions, firmly renewing our aspirations—sometimes every day—and then allow the worst in us to come out?

Christ did not leave us alone in our struggle. He befriended us and pledged to live in us, if we allow him. When St. Paul sins, it is sin acting in him, but when he does the good, he says, "It is no longer I who live, but Christ who lives in me" (Galatians 2:20).

Jesus shares his life with us, and that is the gift we call *divine grace*. He shares his life in many ways, and we receive actual graces throughout the everyday events of our lives.

The ordinary and primary channels of his grace, however, are the sacred "signs" he established in the New Testament and entrusted to the Church. We call them the *sacraments*, and there are seven of them: Baptism, Confirmation, Holy Eucharist, Matrimony, Holy Orders, Anointing of the Sick, and Confession.

A sacrament is, by definition, an efficacious sign of grace, instituted by Christ and entrusted to the Church. A sacrament dispenses divine life to us through the action of the Holy Spirit.

That's the key to understanding the power of Confession. It is not simply a release valve for us when we are beset by anxieties (though it can be that). It is not merely a place to go for advice in a crisis (though it can be that as well). Though it has many natural benefits, its primary benefits are supernatural. Confession is one of God's ordinary ways of drawing near to us—and of drawing us near to him. It is, with Baptism, as St. Jerome pointed out, one of the two doors God has built into his home. It is, as Tertullian said, a beacon established by God to guide us into his heavenly harbor, even as we live on earth.

Without Confession, even the greatest and most virtuous among us feel as helpless as St. Paul, beset by tendencies toward sin and hypocrisy—tendencies we cannot root out with any merely human resources. No drug, no technique, no technology has succeeded in doing what Confession can do: forgive our sins and empower us with supernatural strength to persevere in our struggle to overcome them.

Why go to Confession? Because, God knows, we need Confession. That's why God gave us Confession.

❖ ❖ ❖ ❖ ❖

As we've seen, there are many good reasons to go to Confession. Are there reasons not to go? Well, there are excuses.

Some people excuse themselves, saying, "I'm not a bad person." And that's true. In fact, that's Catholic doctrine and biblical faith. Remember, God created human beings and declared that they were "very good."

But we are created for something very great. The New Testament calls us children of God, friends of God, co-workers of God, brothers and sisters of God, and even "partakers of the divine nature" (2 Peter 1:4). Can we honestly examine our typical days and say that we are living up to all those roles, all the time?

St. John wrote very truly, "If we say we have no sin, we deceive ourselves, and the truth is not in us" (1 John 1:8). Then he raised the stakes by saying, "If we say we have not sinned, we make [God] a liar, and his word is not in us" (1:10).

Jesus came to convince us regarding sin (see John 16:8). He came to save us from our sins (Matthew 1:21). Indeed, the great marvel of our salvation is that *"while we were yet sinners* Christ died for us. . . . While we were enemies we were reconciled to God by the death of his Son" (Romans 5:8, 10; emphasis mine).

If we think we don't need Confession, then we are no better off than Adam, whose obstinate denial destroyed the harmony of God's creation.

In fact, denial of one's own sin is an unhealthy spiritual and mental habit. It is a break with reality, and it has definite social consequences. Even if we delude ourselves by saying, "We have no sin," it is unlikely that our family members, neighbors, and co-workers are so deluded about us. They may be forgiving. They may be patient. But they know our foibles. As the grace of Confession improves our own life, it will have positive effects on theirs as well.

No one is a bad person. God made us good, but our goodness has been wounded, injured, and weakened by original sin. Untreated wounds and injuries don't heal well. They are vulnerable to infection, scarring, and inflammation. What medical care is to the body, Confession is to the soul. It is healing. It gives us grace that makes us whole—to become who we are, to become the persons God created us to be, "in the beginning."

The story of Adam and Eve shows us that none of us is an island. Our actions affect others. God created us as social animals—creatures who need one another. He created us to live in community, and when we wrecked our human community, he redeemed us to live in his Church, a great communion of persons, a communion of saints.

The life of the Church draws us out of ourselves, away from selfishness, and directs us toward others and toward God. The Sacrament of Confession accomplishes this by drawing us toward the Church, toward forgiveness, and toward reconciliation. We are reconciled for communion with God and with others.

This is a need we have by nature. God made us so that the strengths of the community would make up for our individual weaknesses. He entrusted the Church with sacraments that supply our spiritual needs. Though Confession is a private and confidential act, it has profound social consequences.

We need to go to Confession, not just because it's good for "me," but also because it's good for the other people in my life, and it's good for the world we're leaving for the next generation. Remember Adam's fall. Our sins, too, have consequences that we cannot foresee.

God wants us to succeed where Adam failed, and so he has established a ritual way for us to confess our sins. Rituals and routines make life a little easier for us, whether at home, at work, or at Church.

Our goal in Confession is *conversion*—which comes from the Latin word for "turning around." We are turning from self to God.

Sin, on the other hand, is a turning away from God. When we turn from God, we do not turn toward "bad" things. We turn toward created things—pleasures and honors and such. These are good in and of themselves, but we make them bad when we act as if they are more important than God. We sin when we break God's law in order to use created goods by our own standards. This inevitably leads to misery, because God's law is not a set of arbitrary restrictions. It is a path to happiness in the world he created. God didn't impose his law to make us chafe but to guide us to live in harmony with creation. The precepts of the Lord may seem demanding, but they give joy to the heart (Psalm 19:8). Sin may seem the easier path, but it is deadly and a destroyer of peace.

Conversion has been the summons of the gospel since it was first preached in the streets of Jerusalem: "Repent therefore, and turn again, that your sins may be blotted out, that times of refreshing may come from the presence of the Lord" (Acts 3:19).

We go to Confession because we were made to live in the Lord's presence, but we know we're not worthy to live there. Worthiness comes, by grace, with conversion—with the *sacrament* of conversion.

Those who don't have the sacrament often feel they must appropriate it, like the characters in those novels we saw earlier in this chapter. If they cannot seize it, they substitute for it. It is at once moving and saddening to see the number of "anonymous confession" sites available on the Internet. "Completely confidential!" they promise. "No registration required! Simply let it all out and feel good about it!"

The need is genuine, but it is a need as big as God, and no website will give it satisfaction, no matter how many "hits" it may draw. For satisfaction, we need Confession, which God himself established and which alone is efficacious.

From the Pews

I grew up in a Catholic family in which friendship with God was dearly prized. As a child, I learned to speak with God daily in prayer. But sometime in my teen years, I began to reason that the Sacrament of Reconciliation was unnecessary because I could personally go to the Lord and ask forgiveness for my sins.

Throughout high school and college, I continued to attend Mass, pray daily, and take an active part in the Church. I truly tried to live a Christian life, but I found myself increasingly unable to overcome sin. I couldn't understand why God did not help me in my struggles. I began to feel awful about myself as a result of my lack of self-control.

One day I shared with a friend about my difficulties. She didn't preach or even offer advice but only asked, "Do you go to Confession?" Ashamedly, I replied, "No." That simple question weighed on my mind and compelled me to visit my parish church the next Saturday afternoon. As I stood in line for Confession, I felt anxiety welling up: would I remember the right words, the right formula?

When the priest learned how long it had been since I had confessed, he asked, "What happened?" He then led me through a lengthy examination of conscience based on the Ten Commandments. I felt embarrassed that he thought I might have committed all those sins. I was acutely aware of the minutes ticking by, and I dared not look at the other penitents as I walked back to my pew.

Nonetheless, I continued to go to Confession regularly. It was several months later when I realized that I was no longer falling into those sins that had plagued me for so many years. The feelings of worthlessness were gone as well. A huge weight had been lifted. I knew that the change coincided with my returning to Confession, but I had not expected such a dramatic outcome. "Lord, you did hear my prayers after all!" I exclaimed. His help had been there all along, if only I had been willing to receive it.

Today I look back at my return to Confession as one of the major transformational times in my life.

One of the things I used to find difficult about Confession was the embarrassment factor. It was not that I had any earth-shattering sins to confess; it was the embarrassment of repetition that was the stumbling block. Time after time, I would find myself confessing the same sins, and nothing seemed to change. It was while I was mentally tossing this way and that, thinking about my sins and wondering whether I should go to Confession yet again, that God revealed some things to me.

The first thing he revealed was that Confession is not a mechanical action like putting money in a jukebox. Put in your nickel and, hey, presto!—out comes an absolution. God seemed to be saying to me that the core of Confession was not about a set of rules or some tricky process you had to go through to get clean, but was about a person, and that person was Jesus.

The second thing I became aware of was the astounding fact that Jesus loves me. I began to realize that by committing sins, I was distancing myself from Jesus, harming my relationship with him, and stopping the flow of love coming from him into my heart. My sins were damaging, not because I had broken the rules, but because I was shutting out the sunlight of the love of Christ shining on my life.

The next time I went to Confession, a third revelation occurred to me. When I came out after confessing my sins, I felt like a new man. It was, strangely, the same experience I had always had in going to Confession: I go in feeling embarrassed and reluctant to talk about my sins, and I come out feeling as if new power has been put into me. The slate is wiped clean, and I am reconciled to God. Suddenly, I realized that there was real power in the Sacrament of Reconciliation, power to change me, power to combat the evil in my life and enable me to stop sinning and instead to love Christ. It was only after I recognized that power and began to rely on it that I started to see real change gradually taking place in my life, and I began to draw closer to God's infinite love in Jesus.

CHAPTER TWO

THE STORY OF GOD'S MERCY

Do not be ashamed to confess your sins,
and do not try to stop the current of a river.
(Sirach 4:26)

Before we talk more about Confession, we have to take time to reflect on God's mercy. For without an understanding of how much God desires to forgive us, we will not understand why Confession is such a gift.

It's easy to doubt God's desire to forgive us—we may just think that our sins are too great for God's mercy. If so, we should sit down and read the fifteenth chapter of St. Luke's Gospel. Then, when we get to the end of it, we should go back to the beginning and read it again. Since the earliest days of the Church, Christians have found there the key to a rewarding experience of the Sacrament of Confession.

Much of what we know about mercy we have learned from that chapter, and specifically from Jesus' parable of the prodigal son. It is the plainest of stories, recounting a common occurrence. It portrays the most basic human relationships: parent, child, and sibling. It involves the most elemental human emotions. Yet it is profound in its implications, and every inspired word of it carries the weight of many volumes of theology.

Just as the first chapters of Genesis tell us the tragic story of human sin, so Luke 15 relates the amazing story of God's mercy.

The chapter opens dramatically. Jesus is preaching and teaching, and he's attracting a crowd of social pariahs and morally questionable characters—tax collectors, for example, and other sinners. This scandalizes the religious authorities, who expect a righteous teacher to keep better company. They murmur among themselves and gossip about Jesus loudly enough for him to overhear: "This man receives sinners and eats with them" (Luke 15:2).

Jesus doesn't respond directly to them. (After all, they didn't speak directly to him.) Instead, he poses some questions and tells some stories.

He asks them to imagine that they are wealthy herdsmen who own a hundred sheep. If one wandered away, wouldn't you leave the other ninety-nine and go after the lost one? And wouldn't you be happy when you found it? "Just so," he concludes, "there will be more joy in heaven over one sinner who repents than over ninety-nine righteous persons who need no repentance" (Luke 15:7).

He then tells a similar story about a woman with ten silver coins who loses one—and then rejoices when she finds it. "Just so," Jesus says, "there is joy before the angels of God over one sinner who repents" (Luke 15:10).

These are short vignettes, not really stories. They get to the point: God is pleased to recover what is lost.

But Jesus has hardly begun. He goes on, then, to deliver the masterpiece of all his parables.

And [Jesus] said: "There was a man who had two sons; and the younger of them said to his father, 'Father, give me the share of property that falls to me.' And he divided his living between them. Not many days later, the younger son gathered all he had and took his journey into a far country, and there he squandered his property in loose living. And when he had spent everything, a great famine arose in that country, and he began to be in want. So he went and joined himself to one of the citizens of that country, who sent him into his fields to feed swine. And he would gladly have fed on the pods that the swine ate; and no one gave him anything. But when he came to himself he said, 'How many of my father's hired servants have bread enough and to spare, but I perish here with hunger! I will arise and go to my father, and I will say to him, "Father, I have sinned against heaven and before you; I am no longer worthy to be called your son; treat me as one of your hired servants."' And he arose and came to his father. But while he was yet at a distance, his father saw him and had compassion, and ran and embraced him and kissed him. And the son said to him, 'Father, I have sinned against heaven and before you; I am no longer worthy to be called your son.' But the father said to his servants, 'Bring quickly the best robe, and put it on him; and put a ring on his hand, and shoes on his feet; and bring the fatted calf and kill it, and let us eat and make merry; for this my son was dead, and is alive again; he was lost, and is found.' And they began to make merry.

"Now his elder son . . . was angry and refused to go in. His father came out and entreated him, but he answered his father, 'Lo, these many years I have served you, and I never disobeyed your command; yet you never gave me a kid, that I might make merry with my friends. But when this son of yours came, who has devoured your living with harlots, you killed for him the fatted calf!' And he said to him, 'Son, you are always with me, and all that is mine is yours. It was fitting to make merry and be glad, for this your brother was dead, and is alive; he was lost, and is found.'" (Luke 15:11-25, 28-32)

That is our story. We are the children of an indulgent Father. Our Father God has created us to be free and has given us a lavish inheritance. We have misused our freedom and misspent his gifts. By sinning, we have traveled to a "far country" and separated ourselves from our heavenly Father and our heavenly home. Our Father knew where such choices would lead us, yet he gave us the freedom to pursue the life we preferred.

He allowed us to experience, firsthand, the wages of sin.

Only in his abject failure is the prodigal son able to begin an examination of conscience. His motives are far from noble. In fact, they're mostly selfish. We might describe his attitude as "attrition" or "imperfect contrition." But he recognizes, quite clearly, that what he has done is "sin," and that only he is responsible for it. His own sin has driven him to live in filth, abject poverty, and a state of near starvation.

So he decides to go home. Having examined his conscience, he prepares his confession; and as he walks along, he rehearses an Act of Contrition.

It is interesting to observe what happens next. The father catches sight of his son at a distance. Now, if anyone had earned the right to savor the sight of a young man groveling, it was the dad in this parable. Yet he does not wait for his son to drag his sorry body up the driveway. The old man runs down the road to greet his boy. The son begins to make his confession and recite his memorized apology—but his father doesn't allow him to finish! He demonstrates that imperfect contrition is good enough. He shows his willingness to do everything possible to accommodate his estranged child.

That is the way of our Father God. That is the way of the Catholic Church. God does not wait for us to grovel. He does not wait until we've refined our contrition. He meets us halfway—in the confessional. And then he leads us to the banquet table—the Holy Mass.

Jesus' parable acknowledges that this divine indulgence may not sit well with those who are conventionally pious and dutiful in a grudging way. The older brother in the story is no more concerned about "family" than the younger brother was on the day he left with his fortune. The older brother is concerned about himself.

His father, however, wants him to rejoice at the same table as the formerly wayward son. He wants the family back together, better than ever.

A journalist of the last century, April Oursler Armstrong, said that God's "unfairness" was a point of intense struggle for her when she first considered converting to the Catholic faith.

Like many outsiders, I'd been accustomed to think that Catholics had an easy way out. They could do horrible things and go to Confession and be forgiven, and the past was wiped out after a few prayers were said. Outsiders like me, seeing a gangster get a fine Church funeral on the strength of a deathbed or death-row repentance, thought you could get away with murder in the Catholic Church.

It didn't seem fair, that deathbed repentance bit. But when I read the Gospels I found that God didn't play fair at all in the usual human sense. . . . Christ said there was more rejoicing in heaven over the repentance of one sinner than over ninety-nine just men who stayed just. Rather than worrying about being fair, he would remind us that we're supposed to love everyone as we love ourselves, and lovingly want everyone to get the very best, even at the last minute. If we don't love enough for that, we'll lose our own place. It's tricky reasoning for human minds, when love counts more than what looks like justice. But God's ways are not natural to men.[5]

The Sacrament of Reconciliation is the story of God's love, which never turns away from us. It endures even our shortsightedness and selfishness. Like the father in the parable, every time we walk away, God waits, watches, and hopes for our return. Like the son in the parable, all we need to do to return is to recognize our wrong, our need for forgiveness, and our need for God's love.

It remains one of the great marvels of Christ's love that he would make forgiveness so readily available to each of us. In the simple actions of contrition, confession, absolution, and satisfaction, we are restored to a whole new life.

❖ ❖ ❖ ❖ ❖

Confession's *divine* power is an important point for our consideration, for the sacrament can provide a great relief for those who suffer from an extremely sensitive conscience—those who are scrupulous and who worry about the quality of their own contrition. Confession is a bright line they can cross and know, with certainty, that the matter has been resolved.

At the end of the movie *The Sound of Music*, the protagonists, the Von Trapp family, race toward the national border as Nazi patrols pursue them. They know they will be safe the moment they get to the other side of the boundary marker. Confession gives us a similar sense of refuge, a sense of security, a sense that we have crossed from one state (sinfulness) to another and far better one (forgiveness and grace).

Like the prodigal son, our sorrow need not be perfect. Perfect sorrow, known as *contrition*, is motivated purely by love of God, not by fear of punishment or anything else. The human heart, however, is rarely uncomplicated, and our motives are often mixed. That is why our Act of Contrition might sometimes feel like an "act" when we say it, because our love is human and mixed with fear now and then.

Nevertheless, it is good for us to say the traditional prayers. They suggest to our souls the noble qualities to which we should aspire. Over the course of a lifetime, we strive to "grow into" the prayers that we say day after day.

When we go to Confession, we need not enter the confessional with hearts burning with perfect contrition. The

Church teaches definitively that imperfect contrition (sometimes called "attrition") is good enough. In the sacrament, then, Christ makes up the difference. He is the perfect priest; he is the perfect mediator who intercedes on our behalf before the Father. His sorrow for our sins is always perfect, and his sacrifice makes perfect satisfaction for our offenses. (This is the dominant theme in the New Testament Letter to the Hebrews.)

There can be no forgiveness of sin, however, if we do not have sorrow at least to this extent: that we regret offending God, that we resolve not to sin again in this way, and that we make it our firm intention to turn back to God. Our sorrow for what we have done must lead us to the Sacrament of Penance.

God wants to forgive us. Yet he will never violate our freedom, and we can choose to refuse forgiveness. Nevertheless, like the father in the parable of the prodigal son, the Almighty will do everything in his power to bring us safely home. We can trust him to follow through on his own deepest desire. And we can trust him to succeed in his efforts.

From the Pews

"You need to make a good confession." Those were the words of the kind and gentle nun who was acting as my spiritual director as I was coming back to the Catholic Church after a long time away. Sr. Rose, with her warm and welcoming presence, had provided much encouragement and words of wisdom to help me overcome many of the hurdles that stood in the way of my reunion with the faith of my youth. But those seven words struck my heart with fear. I had no idea what she meant by a "good" confession.

In fact, I couldn't remember my last confession, not to mention my first, or recall any instruction during the CCD era of the 1970s that would have prepared me to make a "good" confession. With little or no reference to sin back then, I was ashamed to admit that I didn't know the difference between a venial sin or a mortal one. If Sr. Rose had taken it one step further and mentioned the phrase "examination of conscience," I wouldn't have known what that was either.

Knowing none of what was going on in my head and heart, Sister provided me with the name of a priest. We met at a local retreat house in a comfortable and inviting room. I was immediately drawn to a lovely framed portrait of our Lord. His soft face and probing eyes peered down upon me, and I was completely caught up in the image. Every sin that I had rehearsed flew out of my mind as my heart melted under the beautiful gaze of my Savior communicating so much love, acceptance, and understanding.

Gently, the priest walked me through the sacrament. I don't remember anything I said that day, but I do remember very clearly that when I was all done, the priest said, "You've made a good confession." (How could he have known what Sr. Rose had said to me?)

I learned something that day, and I've experienced it with every confession since: more important than what we have done or have failed to do, what we say or how we say it, is that Jesus meets us right where we are with his perfect mercy and unending grace. He knows *everything* about us and still loves us like crazy. I've also come to realize, more than anything else, that every confession is a good confession because of him.

Confession was so important to my great-grandmother that one day when I was in grade school, she called our home to remind us of an upcoming Penance service. Our whole family went. The next time I remember going to Confession was as a senior in high school. At the time, I felt very weighed down by a "big" sin, and I went into the confessional with the intention of confessing it. However, when I confessed another sin, the parish priest seemed surprised. I became so uncomfortable that I failed to confess the "big" sin and ended up making a bad confession.

A year later, during my freshman year of college, the Holy Spirit led me to Confession once again. While on an architectural sketching assignment downtown, I noticed the Confession schedule posted on the historic cathedral and decided to go. Wearing shorts and a tee shirt and feeling the effects of the heat and my nervousness, my knees stuck to the kneeler. Finally, through the screen, I confessed only the "big" sin—I could think of nothing else.

I will never forget the feeling I had after the priest absolved me. I was in such awe that I nearly forgot my penance! I had walked in with a summer cold, but when I left, I was healed both physically and spiritually. Realizing the power of Confession, I then understood why my great-grandmother thought it was so important.

Today, where I attend Holy Mass, there is always a line for Confession before Mass, reminding me to go more often. As I wait in line, I usually feel foolish for having committed my sins and begin feeling nervous. But kneeling in the confessional, I always meet a merciful Christ. Having confessed with the goal of not repeating that sin, I also receive advice from the priest on not committing the sin again. This sacrament—one of our grace-filled ways to heaven—is now an important part of my life.

CHAPTER THREE

"BY WHAT AUTHORITY?"

Many years ago, I was scheduled to help out at a parish by hearing confessions during the Lenten rush. Lent is the season when the "light is on" at its longest and brightest, and so it's the time when many people choose to come back to the practice of the faith.

As we came into the church but before we had reached the confessional, one man came up to me and told me that it had been thirty years since his last confession. I asked what had kept him away. His answer startled me.

He said, "*You* did."

I was taken aback. I hadn't even been a priest that long. What could I have done as a child or a teenager to scandalize a grown man and scare him away from the sacraments?

My stunned silence made him laugh. He explained that he didn't mean me personally, just the *institutional* Church, which I represented as a clergyman.

He was happy to be home, and I was happy to receive him. Our exchange remained with me, however, and it still gives me pause. As a priest—and now, even more, as a bishop—I represent the Church, and many people will, rightly or wrongly, judge the Church by my actions and words.

A priest, by his character, can give people confidence in the Sacrament of Confession—or he can undermine their faith in the whole business.

"By what authority," people might ask, "do *you* presume to hear anyone's confession and pronounce them forgiven?"

It is a legitimate question. It is good for us as Christians to look to Jesus for the answer. In this chapter, we will examine the salvation Jesus has won for us and how he has arranged for all of us to receive its benefits. We will search out the answer to this unspoken question of so many people who stay away from the sacrament.

"By what authority . . . ?"

Jesus himself faced that question, and as I said, it is a legitimate question. Jesus' opponents rightly pointed out that only God can forgive sins, because a sin is—by definition—an offense against God. Crimes are transgressions against human codes of law, and they are punished or forgiven by human tribunals. Sins, however, are violations of God's law, and God alone is the judge of sinners.

Jesus shocks the scribes when he says to the paralytic, "My son, your sins are forgiven." Then they say to themselves, "Why does this man speak thus? It is blasphemy! Who can forgive sins but God alone?" (Mark 2:5, 7).

Jesus' words would be blasphemy if they were spoken by anyone other than God himself. What the scribes do not recognize is that Jesus is God incarnate. In Jesus the eternal "Word became flesh and dwelt among us" (John 1:14). He is "God with us" (Matthew 1:23). Yet, lacking faith, the scribes see Jesus as merely human and judge him to be a blasphemer.

They are not alone in making that judgment. Later on in St. Mark's Gospel, Jesus tells the crowd, "Whenever you stand praying, forgive, if you have anything against any one; so that your Father also who is in heaven may forgive you your trespasses" (11:25). The scribes are outraged again, and now they are joined by the chief priests and elders. Together they confront Jesus, saying, "By what authority are you doing these things, or who gave you this authority to do them?" (11:28).

We have already seen that Jesus' authority is divine. He took flesh in order to "save his people from their sins" (Matthew 1:21). He proved his earnestness by laying down his life for that salvation. In St. Paul's beautiful phrase, he "*gave himself for our sins* to deliver us" (Galatians 1:4, emphasis mine). "Christ *died* for our sins" (1 Corinthians 15:3, emphasis mine). What more could he have done to prove his authenticity? He was, moreover, vindicated by his resurrection, and he entered the sanctuary of heaven as an eternal priest, offering himself in a once-for-all sacrifice to atone for sins—"a merciful and faithful high priest in the service of God, to make expiation for the sins of the people" (Hebrews 2:17).

We are speaking here of Jesus' work of *redemption*, or *salvation*. He came to save us from a dire situation, from which we could never extricate ourselves. He came to save us from sin and death.

Throughout the Old Testament, the people of Israel offered animal sacrifices to atone for their sins. "Indeed, under the law almost everything is purified with blood, and without the shedding of blood there is no forgiveness of sins" (Hebrews

9:22). Nevertheless, Israel's efforts, though monumental, were ultimately futile. "For it is impossible that the blood of bulls and goats should take away sins" (10:4).

Christ, however, brought the Law to perfect fulfillment and satisfaction. He is the sinless priest, offering his own body, once and for all on the cross, and perfectly and perpetually in heaven. He made satisfaction for every sin committed by humankind, from Adam's to our own.

The perfect offering takes place eternally in heaven, and yet it is begun on earth. In an upper room in Jerusalem on the night before he suffered, Jesus took bread and wine and declared them to be his body and blood. In a recognizably priestly act, he made a sacrificial oblation of himself. He said that his blood "is poured out for many for the forgiveness of sins" (Matthew 26:28). Then he commissioned his apostles to offer the same sacrificial liturgy: "Do this," he said, "in remembrance of me" (Luke 22:19).

With that command, Jesus established what theologians call the "sacramental economy" of the Church. He instituted the Sacrament of the Eucharist, but he also ordained priests who could carry out his priestly action—who would "do this" until the end of the world.

To these same twelve men he had also given other duties, with the corresponding authority to carry them out. After his resurrection, for example, Jesus appeared to the apostles and said to them:

"Peace be with you. As the Father has sent me, even so I send you." And when he had said this, he breathed on them, and said to them, "Receive the Holy Spirit. If you forgive the sins of any, they are forgiven; if you retain the sins of any, they are retained." (John 20:21-23)

He gave them the power to forgive sins in his name—and even to *deny forgiveness* in his name! He was clearly taking a divine prerogative and giving it over to this select group of men. They would forgive God's people, by the power of the Holy Spirit, through the Sacrament of Penance.

Jesus had promised them this power in similarly extraordinary terms. He said to them, "Truly, I say to you, whatever you bind on earth shall be bound in heaven, and whatever you loose on earth shall be loosed in heaven" (Matthew 18:18; see also 16:19). Now that he has risen, he gives them the Spirit, who makes possible what is otherwise unthinkable.

Through the rest of the New Testament, we see the apostles acting with this authority as they exercise discipline over the newborn Church. It is key to the drama that plays out over St. Paul's two letters to the Corinthians.

By what authority did the apostles forgive sins? By Jesus' authority—and by the power of the Holy Spirit.

The power the apostles received was a gift from God, which they in turn passed on to their designated successors. St. Paul said to the young bishop Timothy, "Do not neglect the gift you have, which was given you by prophetic utterance when the elders laid their hands upon you" (1 Timothy 4:14), and "I remind you to rekindle the gift of God that is within you through the laying on of my hands" (2 Timothy 1:6).

This ordination of successors is all part of the same sacramental economy we mentioned earlier. The word "economy" comes from the Greek words for "law of the household." This is the way we live in God's family. These are the sacraments that mark our way as God's Church.

There is, St. Paul says, "one mediator between God and men, the man Christ Jesus" (1 Timothy 2:5), and yet in the same passage, the apostle urges Christian congregations to share in Jesus' office of mediation, offering up their "supplications, prayers, intercessions, and thanksgivings . . . for . . . all" (2:1; see verses 1-5).

In the sacraments, we have the means of mediation—the sources of grace—that Jesus himself established and entrusted to the Church, and so we can go to them with complete confidence. When a priest acts as our confessor, he acts *in the person of Christ*, to whom he has been conformed sacramentally by his ordination. It is not a man who acts; it is Christ who acts. The one who forgives our sins is the eternal Word who took flesh for our sake and gives his flesh for our sake. The power that absolves us of our sins is the same power that created the world out of nothing.

To forgive sins is no small matter, yet for God there is no impossible task. The reliability of the priest—guaranteed by the confessional's seal—is a sign of God's steadfastness. Our trust in the priest is a sign of our trust in God.

The sacraments, by God's will, apply the grace of Jesus Christ in our lives. By this grace we are forgiven. "I confess one Baptism," we profess in the Creed, "for the forgiveness of sins." And Baptism indeed has that power. As Ananias told Saul, "Be baptized, and wash away your sins" (Acts 22:16).

Baptism washes away the stain of transgressions great and small. Scripture makes a distinction between different types of sin: "If any one sees his brother committing what is not a mortal sin, he will ask, and God will give him life for those whose sin is not mortal. . . . All wrongdoing is sin, but there is sin which is not mortal" (1 John 5:16-17). Thus, Christians from the first generation distinguished between "mortal" sin and "venial" sin. St. John made clear that mortal sin puts an end to one's life of grace. Venial sin weakens one's hold on that life.

It is difficult to simply list actions that are mortally sinful. Certain sins would be considered "mortal" under one set of circumstances and "venial" under another. The Church teaches that a mortal sin has three components: the object is a grave matter; the sinner possesses full knowledge that the act is sinful; and the sinner gives full consent of the will. "Grave matter" would include such things as directly taking an innocent life, bearing false witness under oath, or an act of blasphemy against God. Mortal sins plunge us into a darkness that is incompatible with the life of grace: "He who says he is in the light and hates his brother is in the darkness still. . . . He who hates his brother is in the darkness and walks in the darkness, and does not know where he is going, because the darkness has blinded his eyes" (1 John 2:9, 11).

Yet in Baptism, even the most deadly sins are washed away.

Mortal sins committed after Baptism must (under ordinary circumstances) be confessed in order to be forgiven. They require sacramental Confession.

While Holy Communion takes away all of our venial sins, we must never approach the Eucharist if we are guilty of any mortal sin. St. Paul laid this down for us: "Whoever, therefore, eats the bread or drinks the cup of the Lord in an unworthy manner will be guilty of profaning the body and blood of the Lord. . . . For any one who eats and drinks without discerning the body eats and drinks judgment upon himself" (1 Corinthians 11:27, 29).

The apostles exhorted their congregations to call upon the presbyters—call upon a priest—and confess their sins (see James 5:15-16). The apostles' successors echo that summons down to our own day. "If we confess our sins," said St. John, "[God] is faithful and just, and will forgive our sins and cleanse us from all unrighteousness" (1 John 1:9).

God has come to save his people from their sins. That was Jesus' mission. Forgiveness is a very great gift, but even that is merely a precondition for something greater. The greater gift is God's own life. Through the sacraments, we become "partakers of the divine nature" (2 Peter 1:4).

As if it's not enough for us to be snatched from hell, God has made us to live with him in heaven! He has redeemed us to live the divine life—to lives as "gods" (John 10:34), as children of God (1 John 3:2).

Sometimes you may hear people say, "I get my forgiveness on my own. I don't need to confess to a priest." We should indeed ask forgiveness of God for our sins. Our prayer life is incomplete without a brief daily examination of conscience and prayer of contrition.

Nevertheless, Jesus established the sacrament so that we would use it. He told the lepers, "Go and show yourselves to the priests" (Luke 17:14), and sin affects us far more deeply than leprosy.

Already in the ancient Church, there were some who called themselves Christian but resisted the customary way of seeking forgiveness. St. Augustine urged them to get over their inhibitions, for their own good. He said:

> Do penance, as it is done in the Church, so that the Church may pray for you. Let no one say: "I do it secretly before God. God knows it, and he'll forgive me, because I'm doing penance in my heart."
>
> Was it said for no reason, then, "whatever you loose on earth shall be loosed in heaven"? Have the keys been given to the Church of God for nothing [Matthew 16:19]? Do we frustrate the Gospel and the words of Christ?" [6]

When we go to Confession, we can be certain that our sins are forgiven. We have it on good authority. In fact, we have it on divine authority.

From the Pews

I grew up attending many different Protestant churches, and there were many advantages—great Bible studies, for one thing, and amazing potluck dinners! But one of the disadvantages was a definitive lack of certainty that the sins one struggles with can ever truly be forgiven. I can vividly remember trying to come to grips with the sinful actions of my life, only to still feel guilty regardless of my scrupulous apologies. I wanted to know that what I had done was truly forgiven, but I always felt that whatever act of restitution or self-loathing I applied was not bringing about the freedom I longed for.

When I entered the Catholic Church, the Sacrament of Reconciliation was exactly what I was longing for: a true encounter with Christ where I could hear the words of absolution ensuring my forgiveness.

I can still remember my first confession just before entering the Catholic Church. The priest was an older man who sat and listened patiently to things I had never been able to share with any other living soul. My heart was so heavy with guilt and fear, and yet not one word of condemnation found its way into that confessional. The priest patiently listened to every neurotic sin I could remember and lovingly allowed me to leave with the weight of the world literally off my shoulders.

Jesus knew that we would need to hear definitively that we are forgiven, and so he intentionally offered his followers the opportunity to name our sins aloud and hear his words of healing. I know many people who have found such vulnerability before a priest to be terrifying, but for me, it was what I had most wanted. The Sacrament of Reconciliation took me out of my head, away from my second-guessing and attempts at proving to Jesus just how sorry I was.

When we ask Jesus to forgive us our sins, he truly does not withhold his mercy. We can feel the same when we leave, but Confession gives us a certainty that we are truly cleansed from our sins. Why? Because it is Jesus who is truly forgiving us, and that is why the priest doesn't say that he forgives us as a representative of Christ. The priest says "I," and this personal pronoun is Jesus himself. What an amazing gift we have been given in this sacrament!

CHAPTER FOUR

THE GRACE OF REPENTANCE AND CONVERSION

When a priest is wearing "the black," people assume he is on duty. And he is, no matter where he is. People who haven't darkened a church doorway since their first Communion will take the opportunity, when they find it, to ply Father with questions about the faith. You can be sure that Father doesn't mind. That's one reason he wears his distinctive garb.

I was wearing mine as I stood in line at an airport one day when the man standing next to me asked if I could explain something to him. He was about thirty-five years old. He said that he had been raised a Catholic, "more or less," and he remembered that Catholics "do something that helps them get rid of all the excess baggage they carry around, so that they can start again brand new."

I said he was probably thinking about the Sacrament of Confession. He replied that he knew there was something like that; he just did not know how to use it. No one had ever told him, nor had he made much use of the Catholic way to "get rid of excess baggage."

The young man at the airport is not alone—in his curiosity or in his incomprehension and inexperience. Our contemporaries, as I have said, were not raised in a golden age of Christian education. Many people have only a vague notion of what the Church means by "Confession." And yet all of us, at times, carry a great deal of "baggage" that we would like to unload. Despite our best intentions, each of us has experienced personal failure.

This probably accounts, at least partially, for St. Peter's great success in his first effort as a preacher. His message was simple: "Repent" (Acts 2:38), and the Church "added that day about three thousand souls" (2:41).

Peter showed the people the Church's way to check baggage, and they were ready to stand in line.

Some people act as if the Church's call to repentance is an annoyance. They complain as if the Church were trying to impose rules that people neither need nor want.

The truth, however, is that most (if not all) people want a better life for themselves. Sometimes they identify "better" with the quality of their gadgets and the quantity of their possessions. They feel a deep desire for change in their lives, and they think that change means an increase in stuff.

Age often brings a measure of wisdom, and we come to see that the transformation we really desire has little to do with money or status. It has everything to do with what we keep inside of us: our integrity, our morals, and our relationships, especially our relationship with God. If we're honest with ourselves, we recognize that these are the things that need to change.

That moment of realization can trigger the grace of repentance. Repentance is a sorrow for sin that leads to a conversion of life. It's not about "feeling bad" or "feeling guilty"—those are just symptoms that can help us identify the particular disease of the human condition that afflicts us. But we don't stop there. We recognize symptoms so that we can seek a cure. We recognize our sins so that we can repent of them and enjoy peace through conversion of life.

Conversion is another concept that is much misunderstood today. Many people equate it with "changing religions," as when a non-Christian goes through the Rite of Christian Initiation for Adults and "converts" to Catholicism. That's one kind of conversion, but it affects a relatively small group of people.

Many people think of conversion as being an emotional experience—a passionate act driven by inner necessity. Sometimes conversion does happen that way, but not always.

Others think of conversion as an intellectual process—something arrived at by means of study, argument, and the deep engagement of doctrinal and theological issues. Again, each of us may go through such a phase in life, but our conversion entails much more than that.

For a Catholic, conversion is not the matter of a moment. It's a way of life. And it's not a matter of one or another corner or component of life—our emotions, say, or our intellect. It's all-encompassing.

Conversion, for a Catholic, is not like a change of address or political affiliation or wardrobe. Our purpose in life is to be transformed *into Christ*. We want to have the mind of Christ (1 Corinthians 2:16), be the body of Christ (1 Corinthians 12:27), share the blood of Christ (1 Corinthians

10:16), bear the name of Christ (Mark 9:41), have the Spirit of Christ (Romans 8:9), exude the aroma of Christ (2 Corinthians 2:15), and even feel with the affection of Christ (Philippians 1:8).

When I think of my own life and compare it to that goal, conversion seems a daunting task. It would, in fact, be impossible if we did not have the assurance of the grace of Christ (Galatians 1:6).

Long experience also gives me hope. I have been alive long enough—and have been a pastor long enough—to know that people can change.

God extends an offer. He gives us the grace of repentance and the means of conversion. In the ordinary life of the Church, through the sacraments, God gives us all that we need to attain maturity in Christ, the "measure of the stature of the fullness of Christ" (Ephesians 4:13).

What does the Church offer us to encourage us and help us to grow? What are our means of conversion?

In the Church we have access to a tradition that reaches back thousands of years. Practically speaking, that means we have useful protection against unhelpful spiritual fads that come and go. We draw instead from practices that were given by Christ to the apostles and then were developed carefully over the centuries, as the faith came into contact with many cultures. Our methods of prayer and penance have been tested and proven by millions of faithful people over the course of many lifetimes. Our practices have been confirmed as successful by the lives of the saints, who went to their afterlife by way of the Church's basic spiritual path. Along that path, Confession and Communion are the constant mile markers. These sacraments are the ordinary means, established by Jesus himself, by which we come to share his life.

Faith calls us to "frequent" these sacraments—to take *frequent* advantage of them —as our basic course of conversion to Christ.

It is not enough to have a pious wish to love God. Jesus said, "If any man would come after me, let him deny himself and take up his cross daily and follow me" (Luke 9:23). Take special note of the verb "take up" and the adverb "daily." God does not want us to be passive souls. He expects us to respond deliberately with action—and then to respond anew every day.

It's good that the Church has something waiting for us when our "baggage" becomes unbearable. It's good when people perform the minimum the Church asks by going to Confession once a year. But why settle for the minimum when Christ offers us so much more? Why just cling to life when Christ wants us to be fully alive?

This is the constant message of the saints. Read the great masters of the spiritual life—St. Francis de Sales, St. Teresa of Avila, St. Alphonsus Liguori. Not one of them counsels us to visit the confessional only occasionally, only when we feel like going. They urge us to make a *habit* of Confession. They tell us to go regularly and often.

How often should we go? It's an interesting coincidence, but all three of the saints listed above recommended weekly

Confession. They assume, moreover, that anyone who comes to know the joy of the sacrament will want to go even more often! All three saints advise their readers to temper their desires and *limit* Confession to once a week.

In his Wednesday General Audience on November 20, 2013, Pope Francis revealed that he goes to Confession every two weeks: "Even the Pope confesses every fifteen days, because the Pope is also a sinner."[7]

A journalist once asked Blessed Mother Teresa of Calcutta, "Even you, do you have to go to confession?"

She responded, "Yes, I go to confession every week."

This shocked the man—and frightened him. "Then God must be very demanding if you have to go to confession."

She shook her head and explained, "Your own child sometimes does something wrong. What happens when your child comes to you and says, 'Daddy, I'm sorry'? What do you do? You put both of your arms around your child and kiss him. Why? Because that's your way of telling him that you love him. God does the same thing. He loves you tenderly."[8]

Weekly Confession was, for Mother Teresa, all about conversion. It was about turning and becoming like a little child before her heavenly Father.

Many today suggest going to Confession at least once a month. If we go less frequently, it becomes more difficult to track our growth. It's far easier to make a confession after a week than it is after a year. And Confession becomes more satisfying with practice.

It is good to have a standing appointment for Confession. It is ideal if we go regularly to the same confessor. Confession will always be as anonymous as we want it to be, and no confessor may ever disclose what he hears in Confession. Still, there are advantages to developing a relationship with a confessor who knows us well enough to guide our soul and knows whether we are progressing or regressing.

A confessor who comes to know us will know the bad habits and temptations that stand between us and happiness. He can watch for patterns. He can also help us trace our sins back to a dominant fault. If we set ourselves—with our confessor's help—to taking out that root, we'll find our lives free of many of the things that disturb our peace at work and at home. We won't be just dumping baggage anymore. We'll be traveling light and enjoying the trip.

Conversion is a necessary part of the Christian life—it's not optional. Listen to Jesus: "Truly, I say to you, *unless you turn* and become like children, you will never enter the kingdom of heaven" (Matthew 18:3, emphasis mine). The Latin Vulgate translation uses the word *conversi*, meaning "converted," for "turn," describing a turn for the better.

People who don't understand Confession, or who practice it infrequently, will sometimes speak of it as a dark, burdensome, oppressive thing. They treat Confession as they would an unpleasant medical procedure—something to be avoided unless it's absolutely necessary.

It can indeed be painful to admit that we've been wrong. It can be embarrassing to disclose the vices we'd rather keep covered up. But the plain truth is that it's more painful *not* to make the admission. It's far worse to keep things bottled up inside us. There's the wisdom of experience in the famous poem of William Blake:

> I was angry with my friend;
> I told my wrath, my wrath did end.
> I was angry with my foe:
> I told it not, my wrath did grow.[9]

Please don't get me wrong. I am not an advocate of turning one's inner life into a reality TV show. I'm not saying we should share our faults publicly with anyone who is on hand to hear them. No, that is not the Catholic way. While some of the early Christian communities practiced penance publicly, the Church soon established privacy as the norm.

Unburdening oneself in the privacy of the confessional can be a tremendous relief—and it costs nothing more than a brief moment of humility and fortitude.

Confession, practiced regularly, becomes a safe place in our lives. It is a place where we can go when we've complicated life—by indulging our anger, fear, or sensuality. Privacy, secrecy, and anonymity make the confessional the one place on earth where we can always speak with total freedom, receive the counsel of a trusted guide, and then depart with the grace of God.

It's often said that sunlight is the best disinfectant. That's true as well of the light that's on in the confessional. In that light, fears spoken aloud for the first time often dissipate.

Anger finds expression—and resolution. Many of our "demons" flee when we release them into the fresh air of the sacrament. God begins the process of untangling and simplifying our lives, making us more like Christ.

In conversion we turn to Jesus Christ. We become more like him because we can look at him unashamed. As we look to him, "We shall be like him, for we shall see him as he is" (1 John 3:2).

When we "turn," as Jesus said, we become like little children. The Sacrament of Confession is a doorway to the carefree innocence of spiritual childhood. When we confess our sins, we begin to leave behind the things that tangle our thoughts and get in the way of our relationships. Penance frees us to become trusting children of our Father God. When we let go of the sinful past, we can live with serenity in a present moment that is a foretaste of heaven.

That is the ultimate goal of conversion. Jesus saves us *from* our sins, but he saves us *for* something far better. Cleansed from sin, we can live with a clean conscience in the "glorious liberty of the children of God" (Romans 8:21).

From the Pews

Over the years, I went to Confession only two or three times a year. Maybe I held some unconscious resentment toward a priest decades ago whose reception I described to someone back then as "hostile." It was an unpleasant memory of long ago, but I was hesitant to gamble too often by going to Confession more than required by the Church. After all, couldn't I just tell Jesus my sins at home?

During Lent this past year, I resolved to go to Confession every week. I am acquainted with people who say that frequent confession is a big part of their lives. I decided that it is a gift of our Church, so why not give it a chance myself? Practical obstacles made it difficult to go every week, but I did go four or five times during Lent, and I have continued to go much more frequently since then.

The months that have followed have been quite amazing. I have prayed through some life-changing decisions, and I am certain that the grace I receive in the sacrament has played a role in helping me to have a "clean slate" as I listen for God's will in my prayer. And God has given me brand new work and a new direction in my life. How much has the Sacrament of Reconciliation played a part in my life? I believe it has been essential to staying close to the Lord and allowing me to have an "ear to hear" his will for me.

Looking back, I wonder if I was too hard on my confessor years ago. After all, in the last few months, I have not always had an experience to "write home about," but God has *always* given me grace that makes me grateful that I went. And I have come to value my examination of conscience before each confession. I search for sins and sometimes have trouble remembering specific things, but the clarity I get looking through this window has borne fruit in my life.

The advice I get from the priest in the confessional is sometimes surprising and always helpful as I go back out and try to "sin no more." And God's grace makes me a little stronger to face the same habits with more success the next time.

Most of all, the prayer of absolution reminds me of Jesus' total love for me and of his great sacrifice on the cross. I am forgiven! As I gaze at the crucifix while praying after confession, it gives me a profoundly grateful heart. I feel Jesus' arms around me and I know that he wants *my* embrace. I feel most worthy to do just that after I have received the special grace through this sacrament. Then I walk outside with confidence to continue his work in building his kingdom on earth.

I am a stay-at-home mom of six children, ages four to eighteen. Having a large family, I try to schedule certain cleaning jobs regularly so that the house does not get out of control. For instance, every Monday I clean all the bathrooms in my house.

Many times when I am doing these once-a-week jobs, the Lord reminds me, "You schedule your bathroom to be cleaned once a week—why not your soul?" I feel as if the Lord has whispered this message to me many times. I like my car to be crumb free, so I try to vacuum it regularly. I even clean my coffeepot with vinegar once a month. As I am puttering around my house, the Lord gently reminds me, "What about you? When are you going to see me?"

I love Confession because I notice that when I go regularly, I am the best version of myself. For example, I am more receptive to the gentle promptings of the Holy Spirit. When I have taken too long to go, it seems like a bigger job to get to Confession, and I feel like I don't know where to begin because I feel so "messy."

The Lord is so kind and merciful, even when I take a longer than usual time to come to him. Many times it will be weeks before I can make it to Confession, and when it is finally my turn with the priest, I feel edgy and sometimes don't know where to begin. I feel this way many times in my house. I look at the loads of laundry, the dishes in the sink, the dirty floor, and I think to myself, "Where do I begin?" or "It is so messy, I just want to stay in bed!" But the Lord is so kind; no matter where I begin, I feel that he is so pleased that I am moving forward. I am handing him my "sponge" and letting him clean my soul.

Chapter Five

The Fruits of Confession

When the dream of being a rock-and-roll star was very new, the singer Dion fulfilled it.[10] He was one of the first of that generation who dominated the airwaves with Elvis Presley. Born into a working-class family in the Bronx, he was barely out of his teens when he had sold millions of records and had made a fortune.

Nothing, however, had prepared him for fame and all the temptations that come with it. His family was Catholic, but their practice was on and off, and he had never made a habit of Confession.

Like many others who achieve stardom, Dion found it difficult to cope with the pressure. He basked in the attention but resented the intrusions of his privacy. He bought expensive cars, furniture, and clothes. He used expensive drugs that were supposed to make him feel good. Instead, he found himself unhappy and dissatisfied. When he experienced the sudden deaths of several friends, he faced the ultimate questions; but when he couldn't answer them, he just increased his drug intake.

He kept recording hit songs, but his life was spiraling downward. Eventually, he recognized where he was headed. He left the alcohol and drugs behind, checked into a twelve-step recovery program, and joined the nearest church, which was not Catholic.

His life improved greatly. Yet he still felt restless. He was, it seems, carrying around all the "baggage" of the years in which he had been indulging his pride and whims, no matter what effect they had on other people.

From some dim memory of his childhood, he knew what he had to do. He knew of a place where "the light was on" for him. He took a cab to his old neighborhood and rang the doorbell of the rectory at the parish church. He asked the priest, Fr. Frank, if he would hear his confession. The priest agreed.

Dion hardly knew where to begin and stumbled around a bit, until Fr. Frank interrupted him and told him to stand up. Dion did, and the priest hugged him and said, "Welcome home."

That opened the floodgates. The rock star, after many decades on the road, left his baggage at the church. He confessed the sins of a misspent life. And afterward, he made a habit of Confession.

He credits his return to the practice of the faith with a creative breakthrough in his music. A critic recently noted that Dion is the only member of rock's founding generation who is still writing new music. Dion says, "It's God—God and a clean conscience"—that makes him free and makes the music possible.

The fruits of Confession are manifold and profound. We experience them primarily in the order of grace. Sometimes we notice an immediate improvement in our prayer. Sometimes we sense renewed strength in our moral struggles—against gossip, say, or a negative attitude, or a critical spirit.

When the English writer G.K. Chesterton became Catholic, he had to endure the taunts of his friend, the atheist playwright George Bernard Shaw. "You will have to go to confession next Easter," Shaw wrote to him, "and I find the spectacle—the box, your portly kneeling figure . . . all incredible, monstrous, comic."[11]

Chesterton took it in stride and, in his autobiography, made a response. "Well, when a Catholic comes from confession," he wrote, "he does truly, by definition, step out into that dawn of his own beginning. . . . In that dim corner, and in that brief ritual, God has really remade him in His own image. . . . He may be grey and gouty; but he is only five minutes old."[12]

Shaw's point still has its comic effect. The image of the rotund Chesterton as a newborn baby remains amusing. But it's true: Confession is a new beginning, a fresh chance at life. The "child" who emerges from the confessional emerges with new vision.

Another twentieth-century playwright, the absurdist master Eugene Ionesco, ducked into a confessional when he was a young man and feeling his first flush of literary fame. He confessed a number of sins randomly, as if they were not related to one another. But the priest detected a root cause and asked him, "Do you believe in Christ, my child?"

Ionesco responded that he did.

"Well my child, do you believe and accept fully that Christ is God and Creator of the world and us?"

At that point, the young Ionesco wept, because he recognized that his faith was shallow. His response echoed the words of the Gospel: "I believe; help my unbelief!" (Mark 9:24).

The priest replied, "If you really believe, then all corrects itself."[13]

Ionesco discovered that his dominant fault was his weak faith, and he was able to focus on that. It was a pivotal moment in his life. He recognized that if he lived with a deeper sense of his identity in Christ and a stronger sense of God's presence, he would not fall so often into sin.

Confession can lead us beyond a superficial examination of our lives and of the world. Until we make a good confession, we often don't know what we're missing.

A common experience of the penitent is a sense of liberation. To be restored to life as a child of God is to be truly free.

St. Elizabeth Ann Seton converted to Catholicism as an adult, and as she prepared to be received into the Church, she looked to her first confession with dread and fear. Immediately after it was done, her former dread seemed silly to her. She seemed giddy as she wrote to a friend named Amabilia Filicchi:

> It is done! Easy enough; the kindest, most respectable confessor is this [Father] O'Brien, with the compassion and yet firmness in this work of mercy which I would have expected

from our Lord Himself. Our Lord Himself I saw alone in him, both in his and my part of this venerable sacrament! For, oh, Amabilia! how awful those words of unloosing after thirty years of bondage! I felt as if my chains fell as those of St. Peter at the touch of the divine Messenger. My God, what new scenes for my soul![14]

It is easy to see how a soul could grow to love the sacrament. St. Damien de Veuster, a Belgian priest who ministered to lepers on the Hawaiian island of Molokai, had to depend on visits from his bishop in order to make his confession. Once, as Damien waited at the dock for his bishop's boat to arrive, the captain of the boat refused to let the bishop disembark. The government had ordered a strict quarantine of the island. Damien was not to be deterred. From the dock he shouted to the bishop, who was standing on the upper deck: "Bishop, will you hear my confession from here?" The bishop consented, and Damien proceeded to shout his sins aloud, to the astonishment and edification of everyone nearby.

Not everyone is St. Damien, of course, and I suspect most Catholics would have chosen to wait for Confession till the quarantine was lifted!

Yet all sorts of Catholics make the demand. At the opposite end of the spectrum from St. Damien is Rudolph Franz Hoess, who was the Nazi commandant of the Auschwitz death camp. He was ferociously committed to Hitler's cause and gave himself unflinchingly to the task of exterminating people the Fuhrer considered "subhuman"—Jews, Gypsies, Poles, Catholic priests, and men, women, and children who were disabled in any way. In order to "set an example" for his troops, Hoess used to watch from a window while his victims writhed and suffocated in the gas chambers. It was he who condemned Maximilian Kolbe, a Franciscan priest who was later canonized, to die slowly of starvation and dehydration.

Hunted down and imprisoned after the war, Hoess was unrepentant at his trial. He made excuses for his actions. He insisted that he had acted in good faith. He justified everything by saying he was simply following orders. Confronted again and again, he seemed oblivious to the horror of what he had done. He described himself as "a normal man."

Sentenced to the gallows, he awaited his death, and he continued to keep a journal filled with self-justification. Then suddenly one day, as if in a flash, he recognized the full horror of what he had done. "In the isolation prison," he wrote,

> I have reached the bitter understanding of the terrible crimes I have committed against humanity. . . . I have realized my part in the monstrous genocide. . . . I caused humanity and mankind the greatest, and I brought unspeakable suffering particularly to the Polish nation. For my responsibility, I am now paying with my life. Oh, that God would forgive my deeds![15]

He ended his journal entry with a prayer that all future generations would learn from his crimes so that they would never be repeated.

Still, he knew his repentance was far from complete. He begged his keepers to bring in a priest to hear his confession.

In their mercy, they complied, calling in a Jesuit from Krakow, and Hoess was reconciled to God shortly before his execution.

If ever our sins seem so great that they make us hesitate to approach the sacrament, we should contemplate the end of Rudolf Hoess. He was the murderer of millions of human beings, loathed almost universally, and yet the Church waited in God's name to welcome him home when he was ready to repent.

Someone might ask: did the commandant of Auschwitz really *deserve* to enjoy the fruits of Confession, after all he did?

The answer is clearly, "No, he didn't." And neither did Damien of Molokai, Teresa of Calcutta, Dion of the Bronx, or Eugene Ionesco. Frankly, neither do you and I.

The fruits of Confession always arrive as a grace, a gift, unmerited and undeserved. Whatever small penance we perform is merely symbolic. It does little to offset our offenses against God, who is all good and deserving of all our love. We cannot earn God's forgiveness, and we cannot overcome sin by our efforts. We leave those tasks to God when we go to Confession.

We remember the good thief, who misspent his years but repented as he hung dying beside Jesus on a cross (Luke 23:42-43). To him Jesus pronounced words of absolution that we all hope to hear one day: "Truly, I say to you, today you will be with me in Paradise."

Now *that* is the Good Shepherd who leaves the ninety-nine sheep to go in search of the one that's lost. That is the Lord who rejoices more "over one sinner who repents than over ninety-nine righteous persons who need no repentance" (Luke 15:7).

That is the God who leaves the light on for us in Confession. He waits to give us mercy, healing, peace, joy, strength, self-knowledge, clarity, and love. He waits, in fact, to give us everything he has.

From the Pews

A few years ago, my husband and I were asked to help out at a young adult retreat. Prior to the retreat, I had been reading and meditating on the Gospel of Luke. For some reason, I had focused on the crippled woman who was healed by Jesus (Luke 13:10-13).

On the first day of the retreat, I noticed a very beautiful girl who looked like she was sick and in pain. She was hunched over, and she didn't smile or look at anyone. Her eyes focused only downward.

The presiding priest gave a talk on God's love, and after the talk he asked me if I would go and speak to this young woman to see if I could help her in any way. I took her to an adjoining room. As soon as we had gotten through the door, she started crying. She cried and cried for a long time, and then she blurted out, "I had an abortion two years ago and haven't told anyone. I have been in agony ever since." Then more tears.

I just held her. I told her how much God loved her and that this was a very blessed moment in her life. As she continued to sob, I also told her that now she must go to Confession and that God would absolve her of her sin and set her free from this burden she had been carrying. She was a bit scared, but she did agree to go.

After her confession, this beautiful girl left—but she left a different person. She was no longer hunched over; she stood tall and was smiling. This young girl believed that she had been loved and forgiven in the Sacrament of Reconciliation. She had experienced God's mercy.

Like the crippled woman in the Gospel, Jesus had touched her, changed her, and set her free.

I was so mad at God. Why wasn't he helping me out of this tough position that I was in? I felt like it was all just too much for me to handle.

I tried not to show it to anyone. I continued to laugh, smile, and walk the Catholic walk: I went to Mass and said my prayers, but I was holding this secret frustration back. It was like a rain cloud that followed me and dampened my joy. I knew that I should go to Confession, but I just didn't want to do it. I guess I didn't have the courage to tell the priest that I was angry with God. I liked to go to Confession only when I had little simple things to confess.

My husband and I happened to be touring a foreign city with a beautiful cathedral. As we walked in, I saw a sign announcing that Confession was being offered. If a priest were in the confessional, I told myself, I would go. But since it was already late afternoon, I relaxed, thinking that no one would be there. As we turned the corner, however, I saw that confessions had not closed for the day and that there was a priest just sitting there. No one was in line. He was just patiently waiting for someone to come in.

This was my sign that I really needed to go.

Out of excuses, I went in to the priest and sat down. When he started to talk, I suddenly realized that he spoke another language. I had learned the language in college and decided to try to do my confession in his language. I stumbled over words and he filled in my gaps with his broken English. Finally, I burst into tears and the whole story poured out. I unveiled, in my sobbing English, my whole struggle with anger against the Lord, and the dear priest nodded knowingly. It got to the point where I couldn't even speak and just sat there numbly crying. The priest, in broken English, assured me that I didn't have to say everything on my heart. He told me that the Lord knew my struggle and that he loved me and forgave me.

With those words, the weight that I had been carrying around—the anger, the worry, the sorrow—was instantly lifted. My shoulders, my back, my head—all felt lighter. I started crying harder, and then I was laughing. Joy was back! I thanked the dear priest for his kindness and went into the church struggling to control my strange outburst of tears and giggles.

With tourists walking around taking pictures of the beautiful cathedral, I hid in a corner of the church and sobbed and laughed until the tears dried up and the laughing calmed to a silly grin.

It was gone. The horrible, painful weight that I had been carrying around was gone. There was an unusual lightness in my soul that made me look at my situation with new hope and love. I knew that my struggles weren't going to suddenly disappear, but I understood what it felt like to have God as my copilot. I felt his tangible love, and I knew that I could confide my deepest angst and he would still pour out his love for me.

CHAPTER SIX

PREPARING FOR CONFESSION

Pope St. John XXIII was an almost preternaturally cheerful man. The world called him the "Smiling Pope," and news photographers loved him. His warmth radiated from the close-up photographs on the covers of the news magazines—*Newsweek*, *Time*, *Life*, and *Look*.

John was pope from 1959 to 1963. Those were the years before the popemobile, and it was customary for the Holy Father to be carried to public ceremonies on a portable throne, the *sedia gestatoria*, borne aloft by twelve burly men, the *sediari*. John's predecessor, the Venerable Pius XII, was a slight man, while John himself was corpulent. Shortly after his election, on a day when the *sediari* had to carry him several times, Pope John said to one of his aides, "They should receive a bonus to compensate them for the increase in papal weight."[16]

Pope John was a man who knew himself very well, and he didn't airbrush his faults or defects. He made it a habit to know himself. Every day he faithfully conducted an examination of conscience, and he urged others to do the same. The practice was high among the "Rules of Life" he outlined for those who want to make spiritual progress. "In the evening, before going to bed," he wrote, "make a general examination of conscience, followed by an act of contrition."[17]

A "general" examination of conscience is a look back on one's day—a review of the day's events during which we measure our thoughts, words, and deeds against the moral law and the demands of our Christian calling.

The examination of conscience is not just self-scrutiny; it is a form of prayer. It is done in the presence of God, and the proper way to begin is by asking the help of the Holy Spirit. We want to see our day, not simply from our own human perspective, but also—and especially—from God's perspective.

This practice is as old as the inspired authors of the Bible. We are rooted in a faith that has always placed a high value on a "contrite heart" (Psalm 51:17). The prophet Jeremiah said to his countrymen, "Let us test and examine our ways, / and return to the Lord" (Lamentations 3:40). In the New Testament, St. Paul insisted that a person should "examine himself" before receiving Holy Communion (1 Corinthians 11:28).

There are many ways of carrying out an examination of conscience. St. Ignatius of Loyola required members of his religious order, the Society of Jesus, to spend weeks in silent meditation getting to know themselves and their particular faults. That's not an option for most of us who live in the world today. For us, the general examination will take place over the course of a few minutes, as the day draws to a close.

We begin it with a prayer. Then we go over the events of the day. People do this in different ways, depending on their circumstances. Some jog their memories by looking at their appointment books, their calendars, or the call logs on their cell phones. The *Catechism* recommends that we consider our day in light of the Ten Commandments, the Sermon on the Mount, or some other scriptural guidelines (1454). In that light, we evaluate our actions and note any that were faulty. (Some people track these in a notebook or data file, to have on hand for their confession.) Finally, we close with a resolution to do better, and then we make an Act of Contrition. We can choose one of several traditional prayers (see Appendix A), or we can just tell our Lord that we're sorry for sinning.

In addition to the general examination, Pope John also recommended that we make a *"particular* examination of conscience."* He wrote, "Before dinner or before supper, or at least before the general evening examination, make a particular examination concerning the best way to rid yourself of certain vices or failings and concerning the acquiring of certain virtues."[18] The particular exam focuses our attention on the avoidance of one *specific* sin or temptation or the acquisition of one specific virtue. It's a way of moving forward. If you've ever played organized sports, you know that it's not enough just to guard your own goal; you also need to score at the other goal, and that means venturing forward.

The general examination provides us with a good defense. The particular examination is our drive toward the goal: overcoming vice and acquiring virtue.

Often, we'll derive our particular examination from patterns we notice in our general examination. When we make our resolutions at night, we may find ourselves saying, *I need to stop gossiping* or *I should try not to dominate conversations* or *I need to be more attentive to the members of my family.* If so, then we've discovered an area where it would be good to mark daily progress—in a particular examination of conscience.

Pope John conducted his particular examination, briefly, every day around noon. He liked to do it at midday so that he would have many hours to correct his course if the morning did not go well.

Like the general examination, the particular examination is a form of prayer, and so it should follow the same pattern: an invocation of the Holy Spirit, a scrutiny of our deeds and actions, a resolution, and an Act of Contrition.

To know oneself, said the philosopher Socrates, is the beginning of wisdom.

The Good Book, on the other hand, tells us repeatedly and emphatically that "fear of the Lord" is the beginning of wisdom (Proverbs 4:7; 9:10; Psalm 111:10; Sirach 1:12). These are not contradictory statements. For God made us to live in relationship with him. We find our most basic identity in our relationship with God.

The biblical phrase "fear of the Lord" describes the awe one feels in the presence of God. It is not the sort of "fear" we might feel before a tyrant or a torturer. It is, rather, the sense that people have when they realize they've fallen in love with someone. There is, I am told, something overwhelming and overpowering about such a realization. It often comes with a sense of unworthiness. Love always arrives, it seems, as an unmerited gift.

God's love is no different. It is only more fearsome in its implications. For God is all good, without any defect, and yet he comes in love to those who have willfully acted to offend him. He comes to sinners. In his short introduction to prayer, Russian Orthodox Archbishop Anthony Bloom wrote that

> meeting face to face with God is always a moment of judgment for us. We cannot meet God in prayer or in meditation or in contemplation and not be either saved or condemned. I do not mean this in major terms of eternal damnation or eternal salvation already given and received, but it is always a critical moment, a crisis. . . . To meet God face to face in prayer is a critical moment in our lives.[19]

Our examination of conscience is our humble acknowledgment of God's role as our divine judge. By the light of the Holy Spirit, we want to discern God's judgments and draw down his mercy into all the dark corners of our lives.

For God does judge us. It would be absurd to claim otherwise. God is all-knowing, and so he sees us as we are, and he knows our weaknesses. He is himself the standard by which we measure right or wrong. For God, simply to see is to render moral judgment.

If God were not a judge, it would make no sense for us to speak of divine mercy. We would be speaking nonsense to say he is forgiving. Why should such a "god" forgive behavior about which he is indifferent? No, a nonjudgmental deity is a contradiction in terms, a fantasy of New Age speculation.

The true God, however, is indeed merciful and forgiving. God loves us in spite of our weaknesses. In fact, he loves us so much that he wants to help us overcome them—and he possesses all the power that we need for the struggle.

He has given us Confession in order to share that power with us—to give it to us as a grace. Tradition gives us the practice of the examination of conscience so that we can make the most of Confession. It is by such habitual practices that we acquire the "contrite heart" so prized in the Scriptures.

By means of the examination of conscience, the spirit of Confession enters our every day. Confession becomes not just an isolated event but part of a pattern of conversion woven by grace through our waking hours.

The light that is on for us in Confession becomes a beacon, lighting up our ordinary circumstances at work, at home, and in our leisure time.

We need this beacon, because we don't like to notice problems in life, especially when they might be our fault. We prefer to pretend that everything is okay and hope that any unpleasantness will just go away. The human capacity for self-deception is rather large.

This is our nature, and it's not going to fix itself. We're all experts at examining the consciences of other people. Yet we have large blind spots in our own behavior. Jesus said:

> "Why do you see the speck that is in your brother's eye, but do not notice the log that is in your own eye? Or how can you

say to your brother, 'Brother, let me take out the speck that is in your eye,' when you yourself do not see the log that is in your own eye? You hypocrite, first take the log out of your own eye, and then you will see clearly to take out the speck that is in your brother's eye." (Luke 6:41-42)

In the examination of conscience, we take the time to look away from our critical evaluation of others so that we can notice the planks in our own eyes.

Unless we make time for taking stock, we are unlikely to recognize our faults—which are probably obvious to others. Unless we make the effort at self-examination, we will probably fall into the self-regarding habits of the Laodicean Christians who are rebuked by Jesus in the Book of Revelation: "For you say, I am rich, I have prospered, and I need nothing; not knowing that you are wretched, pitiable, poor, blind, and naked" (Revelation 3:17).

Good Pope John examined himself daily. He often had to arrive at this conclusion: "Having made a general examination of my behavior during these recent days, I have found good reason to blush and feel humble."[20]

That need not be a conclusion, however, but a step forward—a step along the way that leads to Confession—and that is good news!

Pope John's predecessor, Pope Pius XII, made this remark: "The sin of the century is the loss of the sense of sin."[21]

Pope John's successors, Pope Paul and Pope John Paul II, echoed that judgment—quoting it verbatim—and developed it further still. To sin, said St. John Paul, is to act as if there is no divine judge or judgment in life. Ultimately, it is to deny the possibility of justice. "The loss of the sense of sin is thus a form or consequence of the denial of God. . . . To sin is also to live as if he did not exist, to eliminate him from one's daily life."[22]

Pope John Paul called this attitude by the name of "secularism," and noted that it had come to dominate governments and even the mass media.

Bad ideas sometimes begin with a good impulse. The "loss of the sense of sin" arises, I believe, from a misguided notion of tolerance. Democracies thrive because of a neighborly forbearance of differences of opinion. Tolerance does not, however, require us to abandon our convictions or deny the existence of moral standards. Tolerance does not demand that we call "good" what is evil or "evil" what is good. Nor does forgiveness of an action mean that we approve the action; in fact, we can only forgive something that is a genuine offense.

Conscience is the faculty by which we judge the moral quality of a human action. Conscience moves us to do good and avoid evil. Conscience gives us the light we need to recognize both.

To become indifferent to right and wrong is not to become more "broad-minded." It is, rather, a forfeiture of conscience—and those who forfeit conscience lose the sense of sin (as the popes have noted) and, with it, all moral sense.

We become *more* conscientious, however, as we exercise our conscience and examine it—and as we let our examination lead us to Confession. It makes for a happier and fuller life. Just look at the example of Good Pope John.

From the Pews

I remember the exact place on the street by my home where I said to the Lord, "There has to be something more to my Catholic faith than Mass on Sunday." I was about eighteen. So I began going to daily Mass whenever possible and continued going regularly to Confession, which I had done since I had first received the sacrament at the age of seven.

But still there seemed to be something missing. I didn't realize at the time that what was missing was a personal relationship with God—Father, Son, and Holy Spirit.

But some years later, that all changed through one specific confession. A priest had given me some Scripture verses to read about the Holy Spirit. Almost immediately, the Holy Spirit began bringing to mind different memories of sinful things I had done, said, or thought from my childhood to that present time. When this time of grace first began, I was in bed. So I quickly got a piece of paper and starting writing them down. This happened for a number of nights—more sins surfaced. With the business of my day over, the Holy Spirit was able to show me where I needed to repent. I then made an appointment for Confession.

I began by saying that in one way or another, I had broken all of the Ten Commandments. The priest asked me to be more specific. I have to admit that I've never found confession easy and had in the past been prideful and had chosen not to be too specific when confessing my sins. At this confession, I wanted to be completely humble. I wanted everything to be brought into the light so that I could have a new start with God. I didn't want Satan to have a stronghold in any area—especially guilt. So I decided to hide nothing. I mentioned everything that the Holy Spirit had shown me. Oh, it wasn't easy! I was ashamed and embarrassed to admit some of the things I had done. But grace abounded.

After receiving absolution, I truly felt like a new creation. I knew that all the sins of my past had been forgiven and that I was washed clean in the blood of Jesus. I experienced great peace and the unconditional love of God! The priest then suggested that I recommit my life to God. I chose to do so after receiving Holy Communion the next day. It was the feast of St. Matthew. Jesus said to Matthew, "Follow me" (Matthew 9:9). That day I began a personal relationship with my God. Nothing was missing!

CHAPTER SEVEN

CELEBRATING THE SACRAMENT

The liturgy of the Catholic Church is rich, complex, and beautiful. It is the cumulative work of centuries and bears the mark of influence by many cultures and some of history's greatest minds. Some rites are especially intricate, and the priest who officiates has to keep his place in several books. It can be daunting.

That's emphatically *not* the case for Confession. The ritual could not be simpler, and many of the requirements can be adapted to accommodate circumstances or the needs of different penitents.

Many people feel anxious or self-conscious because they don't recall quite how the ritual goes. Some people worry that their jitters will cause them to miss their cues. These are the most misplaced of worries. Even if a penitent forgets everything or misses every other line, it doesn't matter.

Confession is not a symphony or ballet that requires precision from every player. It moves forward even with interruptions, even with improvisations, and with plenty of back-and-forth. It's scripted but in a minimal way. It is the only rite that is intended to be a conversation.

I have divided the penitent's part into ten "steps," which I'll describe below. That makes the rite sound far more complicated than it actually is. All ten steps are just baby steps, and our confessor is there to guide us if we're unsteady or unsure of where to go.

A famous filmmaker once quipped, "Eighty percent of success is just showing up." That is true of success in Confession as well. Many people put off going because of one anxiety or another. But if they make it to the confessional, then their confessor will surely guide them the rest of the way—to absolution and to an abundance of grace.

Step One: Showing Up

The first step to making a good confession, then, is knowing when and where to show up. We live in an age—thanks be to God—when that information is readily available in many forms.

Most churches list Confession times, along with Mass times, in their weekly bulletins and on their parish websites. Many diocesan websites aggregate this information and enable visitors to search for the most convenient places and times. So we can search by zip code to find the sites nearby. Or we can search by day and hour to find the time slots that suit our schedule. Most of the websites that are not searchable still enable visitors to find Confession times with a few clicks of the mouse.

It's unlikely that all the scheduled times will fail us. But if they do, we simply need to pick up the phone and make a call. Most parishes welcome calls from individuals to schedule an appointment with a priest for Confession.

If we do show up for a parish's standard hours, we should try to arrive early, in case there's a line.

Step Two: Examination of Conscience

This is another good reason to arrive early: it gives us time to gather our thoughts in quiet prayer and prepare ourselves for a thorough and truly contrite confession. If we prepare well, we won't have to do in the confessional what should be preliminary work done in prayer.

The rite itself recommends that we prepare by silent, prayerful reflection, using Scripture as a light to shine on our lives.

A good examination of conscience makes Confession go more smoothly. It also makes the process more efficient, and that's an act of kindness for the people who may be waiting after us in line.

As we noted in the previous chapter, the Ten Commandments or the Beatitudes can serve as excellent reference points for our examination. Both are included in the appendices at the end of this book, as are more detailed questions that relate the Commandments to the conduct of our lives here and now.

Step Three: Enter the Confessional

In most churches, the confessional is a booth with a compartment for the priest confessor and another for the penitent. There may be a light that signals when the penitent's side is occupied or empty. If it is empty, of course, it is available for the next person in line. Some places, however, have no lights, and the signal for availability is an open door. If we're not sure whether the confessional is occupied, we can knock on the door.

Once we enter, we should close the door after us. What we do next depends on the construction of the booth. Some booths give us the option of kneeling behind a screen (for anonymity) or sitting in a chair (to confess face-to-face). In that case, we can choose the option we prefer. Others are constructed solely for one method or the other.

As we enter, Father will greet us or acknowledge our presence. Once we have taken our place, we should make the Sign of the Cross and pray the customary blessing: "In the name of the Father, and of the Son, and of the Holy Spirit. Amen."

Step Four: Reading of the Word of God

This step is optional, and a confessor pressed for time may skip it. If he does read something, it will likely be a very brief passage from Scripture dealing with God's mercy and the call to repentance. All we need to do is listen with an open heart and receive it as a blessing. When the word of God is proclaimed in the liturgy, it is living and active (Hebrews 4:12), and it works in us to powerful effect.

Step Five: Confession of Sins

This is the most important thing we do in the sacrament. If we have prepared well, it should not take long, even if we're covering a long stretch of years.

We begin by saying just how long it has been: "It has been _____ since my last confession." Then we dive right in

with the briefest of introductory words: "My sins are . . . "
We can simply list them off. If we have questions, we can raise
them with Father. If he has questions, he'll ask.

We should strive to make our confession *complete*. We are
required to confess all our mortal sins. We must not intentionally hold any back—or miss any due to a careless examination
of conscience.

It is helpful for us to confess venial sins as well, especially
those that we fall into again and again. The sacrament will
give us the grace to overcome them, and Father may be able
to give us some good practical advice for the task.

We should strive also to make our confession *concise*.
There is no need to go into detail, unless the detail is necessary to show the degree of our guilt. We should avoid the
very human tendency to excuse ourselves by telling the "back
story" to our sins. To be concise is to be charitable too toward
the people who may be waiting in line.

Finally, we should strive to be *clear*. It's okay to be polite
and observe some decorum, but we should still call our sins
by their names. It is possible to be so euphemistic that Father
cannot possibly know what we mean. If we do this intentionally, in order to obscure our actions, we are really withholding
our sins, and that is not a confession at all. A priest cannot
"bind" or "loose" a sin if he cannot tell what it is.

Confessing our sins needn't take long and, in most cases,
shouldn't take long. In Confession, as in all of life, we should
strive for simplicity before God.

When we have finished confessing, we can let Father know
by saying something such as "These are all my sins."

Step Six: Father's Response

Once again, we are on the receiving end, and we need only to listen with an open mind and heart. Father may now speak a word of practical advice. If we have questions, this is a good time to raise them.

After giving his counsel, the priest will assign us some act of "penance," usually a prayer or charitable deed, that will make "satisfaction" for the offense against God. Whatever small penance we receive is merely symbolic. The gravity of an offense against an infinite God is truly incalculable. We can't make up for it. That is why God became a perfect man, to lay down his own life as satisfaction for our sins. When we accept our penance, we "complete what is lacking in Christ's afflictions for the sake of his body, that is, the church" (Colossians 1:24). What was lacking in Christ's suffering? Nothing at all, except what he willed to be lacking so that we could share his life. This we do through the penance Father assigns.

Step Seven: Act of Contrition

Father will invite us to make an Act of Contrition, a traditional form of prayer. There are many ways we can choose to respond. The Rite for the Reconciliation of Individual Penitents (see Appendix A) notes that a penitent may express his sorrow in the words set forth in the ritual "or in similar words." If we want help with the Act of Contrition, we can always ask the priest.

We can simply adapt the *Confiteor* prayer that we know from Mass: "I confess to almighty God, and to you, Father, that I have greatly sinned in my thoughts and in my words, in what I have done and in what I have failed to do, through my fault, through my fault, through my most grievous fault." We may also choose one of the many expressions from Scripture, such as "God, be merciful to me a sinner!" (Luke 18:13). Or we may choose an Act of Contrition from a prayer book. (There is a traditional version in Appendix B at the back of the book.)

The essential thing is to express our sorrow and say it to God. "Contrition" is simply our sense of sorrow for our sins. It is a necessary quality for a valid confession.

The Act of Contrition is very important because sometimes we may not *feel* especially sorry. But by this "act," we are showing God our good faith. We are demonstrating our love by a small deed. We are expressing sorrow as an act of will rather than as an emotion, and that can be a far greater expression of love.

Step Eight: Absolution

This is the moment for which we have been waiting. This is the reason we entered the confessional booth in the first place. After we say our Act of Contrition, Father extends his hands and recites the words that absolve us of our sins. He does this not of his own power but in the name of the triune God.

The rite concludes, rightly, with praise for God. Quoting the beginning of Psalm 118, Father will say, "Give thanks to the LORD, for he is good." And the penitent responds with that famous psalm's refrain: "His mercy endures for ever." People sometimes forget the response, but that is no reason to worry; Father can supply it.

What we should not miss here is the chance to thank God for his mercy. Remember this story from the Gospels:

> As [Jesus] entered a village, he was met by ten lepers, who stood at a distance and lifted up their voices and said, "Jesus, Master, have mercy on us." When he saw them he said to them, "Go and show yourselves to the priests." And as they went they were cleansed. Then one of them, when he saw that he was healed, turned back, praising God with a loud voice; and he fell on his face at Jesus' feet, giving him thanks. Now he was a Samaritan. Then said Jesus, "Were not ten cleansed? Where are the nine? Was no one found to return and give praise to God except this foreigner?" And he said to him, "Rise and go your way; your faith has made you well." (Luke 17:12-19)

In the Bible, leprosy is often used as a metaphor for sin. As contagion makes us dangerous to other people, so sin makes us spiritually "unclean" and unable to enter into God's presence.

To be cured of such an ailment is to regain one's life. And yet, as one of the ancient Church Fathers remarked, to forgive sins is a greater work than to raise the dead. Christ has done something more marvelous for us in the Sacrament of Penance than he did for those ten lepers who were cast out from their village. He has done something greater for us than he did for Lazarus when he brought him forth from the tomb.

We should give thanks, for he is good, for his mercy endures forever.

Step Ten: Performing Penance

Whatever penance Father has assigned, it is best for us to perform it as soon as possible upon leaving the confessional. If we do so, we preserve the integrity of the rite and bring it to a natural closure. Only then, when we've fulfilled our penance, is the Sacrament of Penance complete.

There are also good practical reasons to be prompt. We're less likely to forget to do our penance if we complete it right away, and we're less likely to forget what penance was assigned.

If we make our confession in a church, we can make a beeline from the confessional to the tabernacle, where our Lord is truly present. We can say our prayers and, once again, say "Thank you" to the Lord.

If Father assigned some action that can only be completed later on—say, a charitable work—then we should jot it down so that we don't forget to do it.

As we remember the marvels the Lord has done (Psalm 105:5), his promise is fulfilled: "I will remember their sins and their misdeeds no more" (Hebrews 10:17).

From the Pews

Until the last couple of years, I went to Confession very infrequently. Sometimes I would get anxious just thinking about going to Confession. A pit would start to grow in my stomach as I examined my conscience and was convicted of how I had sinned. And every time I went to receive the sacrament, my heart would start pounding, my throat would start closing, and my cheeks would burn as I entered the confessional.

I felt humbled and stripped bare. I hated my sins, but even more, I hated my own weakness, how frequently I fell into the same patterns of behavior even though I knew they were destructive to my relationships with God and others. Going to Confession made me face my failings once again, and it forced me to let go of my pride and be honest with God and with myself about how I had sinned.

But every time that I humbled myself and confessed my sins, I was met with such kindness and love from God through the priest who spoke the words of absolution over me.

One time in particular, the priest hearing my confession reminded me of the words he would pray over me, of the peace that God gives every time we seek him out in the Sacrament of Reconciliation. There is such freedom in hearing those words: "May God grant you pardon and peace. And I absolve you of your sins, in the name of the Father, and of the Son, and of the Holy Spirit."

I had been harboring unforgiving and hurt feelings toward a few family members, and the priest's words reminded me that I didn't need to feel that way anymore. In confessing my sins, I was laying down that burden, and in return, God gave me his peace and renewed grace to love well.

I cried as I did my penance (as I often do), but these weren't the tears of shame or fear I shed when I was confessing my sins; these were tears of gratitude for the grace I received. He heard and answered my prayer: "Have mercy on me, a sinner" (cf. Luke 18:13).

It was this experience of peace and God's loving mercy that continues to draw me back to the Sacrament of Confession time and again.

I grew up in a family where mistakes were not acceptable and disagreements often ended in silence and bitterness. I was afraid of ever being wrong. And when it came to my faith, I was afraid that my weaknesses and sins would eventually land me in hell. I was legalistic and chained by fear and shame. Thankfully, God knew I needed him to break into my life in a big way.

I went to college a faithful but fearful Catholic. There I met Christians who encouraged me to foster a personal relationship with God. They also prayed that I would receive more of the Holy Spirit. Emboldened and filled with the Holy Spirit, and after much thought and prayer, one day I went to Confession and told a priest about all of my life—my childhood and everything else that weighed on me.

While I was still speaking, I was startled as I began to feel God's love wash over me. I just knew, in the core of my being, that I was loved. Jesus Christ was present in the priest who quietly listened and didn't cut me off or cut me down, which was what I had sometimes experienced when I tried to speak up at home. I still remember the tears streaming down my face; I couldn't stop sobbing. A burden that had built up over my whole life was removed. It was like coming out of the cold and into a warm house. My bones ached with relief.

I can't remember exactly all that the priest said that day, but I do remember that he told me that *God loved me*. That day this truth finally lodged deeply in my heart, and I learned that I didn't have to have everything figured out before I went to Confession, before I asked God for help.

I now go to Confession with much more faith in God's desire and ability to heal and care for me. Confession reminds me that I can ask the Lord for help with anything. I don't have to be perfect; God will forgive my weaknesses and give me the grace to do better. More than anything, I can trust that he will love me—no matter what mistakes I make.

CHAPTER EIGHT

OBSTACLES, REAL AND IMAGINED

When asked why they stay away from Confession, people give many different answers. Some are reasons. Some are explanations. Some are excuses. In this chapter, I'd like to respond to some I've actually heard and some that have been reported to me by my friends and fellow clergymen. Some are very common objections. Others will sound strange, perhaps, but, I assure you, I'm not making any up.

I don't even know when confessions are offered at my parish.

Let's start with the easiest problem to solve. Confession times, as we mentioned elsewhere, are usually posted on the parish or diocesan website and published in the parish bulletin. If your search of those sources proves fruitless, make a telephone call. It will probably take less than a minute.

I don't really have to go. All my sins are venial.

The only sins that must be confessed are mortal sins, but why limit the practice of confession to mere necessity? We only *need* to see a doctor when our life is in danger. We only *need* to see a dentist when we're in danger of losing a tooth. But it's in our best interest to schedule regular checkups and routine tests. Well, it is spiritually unhealthy for us to grow comfortable with our venial sins. Venial sins may not end our life of grace, but they sicken it. They also weaken our resistance to temptation and leave us vulnerable in any near occasions of mortal sin. We cannot build a friendship—or any relationship—if we don't take the time to resolve differences and apologize for offenses. The Church's *Code of Canon Law* makes this clear: "It is recommended to the Christian faithful that they also confess venial sins" (Canon 988.2).

I don't know how to go.

It is a sad fact that an alarming number of Catholics made their last confession at their first confession. That shouldn't matter. Confession isn't like carpentry, neurosurgery, or any other task that requires special skill or training. If we simply show up, the priest in the confessional will be happy to guide us through the process. It is better if we arrive prepared, of course, but there is no shortage of resources for that purpose. Appendix A of this book lays out the rite, and chapter 7 walks through it step by step. Many confessional booths have a handy guide posted inside.

I'm embarrassed. I'm ashamed.

That's a natural feeling, and it can be a healthy reaction to one's own sin, as long as we know what to do with it. Such emotions should move us not to deny the problem, ignore it, or put it off. They should lead us to acknowledge that the problem is sin and that the sin is our own responsibility. Such feelings should lead us to Confession, where we can begin to resolve them.

I would shock Father.

I assure you that by the third anniversary of his ordination, a priest has heard most of the sins that can be confessed. You are not likely to shock him. If you're truly concerned about the effects of your confession, you can always make an appointment with an older, more experienced priest, or even with a prison chaplain. And if your concern is genuine, you probably need to make your confession sooner rather than later.

I could never look Father in the eye again afterward.

Priests are practiced in forgetting. We make it a habit. From our first training in seminary, we are encouraged to do so. The seal of the confessional is a solemn obligation for us, and we do not wish to violate it in any way. The simplest and safest way to keep it inviolate is to make an active effort to leave behind all that's heard in the confessional—to put it out of mind. I assure you that years of experience have sensitized Father to the fallen human condition. He is more aware than you are about the persistence and pervasiveness of sin, even among the good people who are pillars of the parish. You can look him in the eye. He won't look at you differently.

I'll just say, "I'm sorry" directly to God in the privacy of my home.

To be a Catholic is to recognize the role of the Church, not as incidental or secondary to salvation, but as the very means created and given to us by Jesus. Through the sacraments, his saving work—his death and resurrection—is re-presented in our day and applied to us. Jesus gave the power of binding and loosing to his apostles. He established them as judges in the Church, and they passed that authority on to the Catholic clergy in every age. They cannot judge, however, what they do not know. They cannot bind or loose a sin if the sin is not confessed. It's good to make a habit of saying, "I'm sorry" to God, and to do so daily with an examination of conscience and Act of Contrition. But a truly spiritual life—a relationship with God—requires more of us.

I'm at work during my parish's regularly scheduled confessions.

What about the parish down the road? Is its schedule more compatible with yours? Is there a parish near your workplace? If so, have you looked up its schedule? If all these options fail, pick a parish, call the pastor, and make an appointment. It's worth the extra effort.

I got yelled at the last time I went to Confession.

We all have bad days and we all do things we regret. Priests, too, go to Confession because of their personal failings. Please forgive the priest who wronged you and move forward with your spiritual life. We don't allow our teeth to fall out because we fear the dentist. We shouldn't allow one negative experience to keep us from sacramental grace. It's very unlikely that you'll run into the same problem again.

I'm too busy.

I'm sure you are busy. You may indeed be "too" busy. We all make time for the things that are important, and nothing is more important than your spiritual life; nothing is more urgent. Many things at work or home can wait. What's more, the work you do and the busy life you lead will likely go better because you chose to give a half hour to the confession of your sins. When we make things right with God, we can return to our tasks with a newfound serenity. That often makes for better productivity and a happier home.

It's too hard to remember all my sins. I can't remember what I ate for breakfast today.

Examine your conscience and do your best. Father will help you along. If you make a regular practice of examining your conscience—nightly, as we describe in chapter 6—you'll gain a keener sense of your sins, and you'll begin to notice patterns, which you can point out to Father. Frequent confession is the best remedy for this particular strain of amnesia. If we confess monthly, we're more likely to have our sins readily in mind than if we confess yearly.

It's been too long. I'm past the expiration date.

That's funny, but the only expiration date we have is the day we truly expire. The word "expire" comes from the Latin for "breathe out" or die—and yes, after death there is no Confession, only judgment. In the meantime, it's never too late to return to the sacrament. If it's been more than a year since your last visit, you have indeed been away too long. But it's not too late to fix that up and get back on track.

I'm afraid of face-to-face Confession.

Call your pastor and ask if there is another option. Most parishes keep some form of "fixed grille" to comply with the norms of the Church. If your parish doesn't have one, Father will probably know a nearby church that does. Ask.

I'm claustrophobic and I panic in the confessional booth.

Your problem is not as unusual as you might think. In fact, I know of a priest who shares your struggle. He had to make a heroic effort over the course of years to overcome the problem. He succeeded. But you needn't struggle the same way. The priests in your parish can surely accommodate you by hearing your confession in another setting. If you'd still like to keep your anonymity, say so. Many parishes have portable screens that can be used in circumstances like yours. We should not let any fear keep us from the sacrament.

I'm old. I don't sin anymore.

Some people equate "sin" with just one category of sins, or violations against just one of the Commandments. As we grow older, our temptations do change, but we are by nature no less prone to commit offenses against God. Some people, as they age, shift from lust to pride, or from gluttony to envy. The Good Book tells us, "If we say we have no sin, we deceive ourselves, and the truth is not in us" (1 John 1:8). It's likely that a very old man wrote that line. Renew your effort to examine your conscience.

There's too much negativity.

Confession is not primarily about sin but about mercy, just as medicine is not about sickness but about health. If we keep our eye on the goal, if we keep our focus on Jesus, we will maintain the right attitude toward the sacrament. There's nothing negative about conversion. There's nothing negative about healing. There's no downside to putting sin behind us. It's all for the good.

I resent the fact that the Church requires us to go once a year.

Think of it as an opportunity. The problem with us humans is that we don't accept favors from God unless he requires us to accept them! He actually had to *command* his people to take a day off every week, or they wouldn't do it! Try to understand our religious obligations not as impositions but as accommodations of human nature. Several millennia's worth of wisdom has gone into the practices we've inherited.

At Mass, the priest pronounces absolution, doesn't he? In the penitential rite, he says, "May almighty God have mercy on us, forgive us our sins, and bring us to everlasting life. Amen." Doesn't that count?

It does "count," but it's not quite the same thing as absolution. When we receive Holy Communion, we are cleansed of all our venial sins. The very touch of Christ accomplishes our healing. But Scripture warns us of the distinction between venial sin and "sin unto death," or mortal sin (1 John 5:16, KJV). If we sin mortally, we destroy the life of grace in our soul. This renders us unfit for communion with God. The priest's prayer of blessing in the Mass does not apply to mortal sin. Under ordinary circumstances, mortal sin can be forgiven only in the Sacrament of Confession.

I just go to my parish's penance service for general absolution.

It's true that sometimes during Lent, parishes hold communal penance services. These usually begin with a time for individual confession and then proceed to prayers in common and a final prayer of absolution by the presiding priest. That general absolution, however, applies only to the people who have already confessed their sins sacramentally. Priests may also give general absolution to groups of people who are in imminent danger of death.

There is a famous painting of Holy Cross Father William Corby giving general absolution to the soldiers as they went off to fight at Gettysburg in 1863. Many of us were moved to hear the accounts of Father Mychal Judge, who died on September 11, 2001, as he stood giving general absolution to the New York firefighters as they were entering the inferno of the World Trade Center. General absolution is a means of mercy intended for extraordinary circumstances. Confession should be part of an ordinary Catholic life.

From the Pews

I have struggled for my entire adult life with how frequently I go to the Sacrament of Reconciliation. I rationalize about why I can't go on a regular basis. I'm too busy. Confessions are not held at the right time. I have work to do. My family events are more important. I don't like the way certain priests treat people. I haven't killed anyone. I haven't committed any mortal sins lately, so I will wait until the time is right. In short, I'd rather have a root canal than go to Confession.

My struggles came to a head when a very good friend, Alan, died at a young age. It seems that his constant bouts with clinical depression took over at one point, even though he was smarter, wiser, and holier than I will ever be. Before his death, Alan had become totally isolated from others and had even stopped taking his medications. Despair took over and he committed suicide, leaving family and friends like me with overwhelming feelings of guilt. Why hadn't I noticed and stepped in to stop his downward spiral? Why did I let him slide away by not calling him for six months or more at a time? I called our pastor, Fr. Greg, and asked to speak with him about my struggles.

After talking about my loss and the neglect of my friend, I asked to go to Confession. And in the process I admitted my irregular use of this sacrament. I told Fr. Greg that I didn't want to live like that anymore. His suggestion was that I schedule monthly or bi-monthly confession for six months to a year at a time.

It made sense. I would never miss a meeting at work or a business appointment or maintenance on the family car. I could do the same for a reconciling meeting with Jesus. So far, it is working. I have greater peace and am happier about my life and my work. My wife even catches me whistling around the house! That's because I am experiencing the healing power of regular sacramental Confession over and over again. And best of all, I am combating "spiritual amnesia" about how much Jesus Christ loves me.

CHAPTER NINE

A SACRED TRUST:
THE SEAL OF THE CONFESSIONAL

God has always dealt with his people through human representatives who are chosen and called. Out of all the people who lived in ancient Mesopotamia, God called Abram to be the patriarch of a chosen people. Out of all the Israelites in Egypt, God called Moses to be his mediator and lawgiver. Out of all the sons of Jesse, God called David to be king. From the fractured tribes and from the dispersed, God called the prophets. To lead the worship in the Jerusalem Temple, he called the high priest, the priests, and the Levites. In the days when the Temple was standing, the people of Israel would travel to Jerusalem to confess their sins to the priests and offer sacrifice at the nation's only altar.

In the New Testament, God continued this pattern. Christ called forth apostles. Through the apostles, he designated bishops, presbyters, and deacons, each with corresponding duties. To them he gave a sacred trust—the care of his holy people, the Church. To them he gave the power to forgive sins and heal souls.

Chapter 9 of the Acts of the Apostles tells the great story of St. Paul's conversion. Paul (then known as Saul) had sinned grievously by persecuting Christ and his Church. He was an accessory to the murder of St. Stephen. He was on his way to Damascus to wreak further violence on the Christians there.

Jesus initiated Saul's conversion by striking him down and speaking to him from heaven. However, that was not the end of the process but only the beginning. Christ sent another disciple, Ananias, to instruct Saul, give him spiritual direction, and guide him along the sacramental path of the Church.

This is still the way of the Church. God gives us priests, and he entrusts the care of our souls to them. The power to forgive sins in the name of Jesus Christ is a privilege and a duty. It is something central to the identity and self-understanding of a Catholic priest. The more he exercises this faculty, the more he feels fulfilled in his priesthood, in his calling from God, and, indeed, in his life. Hear the witness of Pope St. John Paul II as he looked back on his own experience in ministry.

> The priest is the witness and instrument of divine mercy! How important in his life is the ministry of the confessional! It is in the confessional that *his spiritual fatherhood* is realized in the fullest way. It is in the confessional that every priest becomes aware of the great miracles which divine mercy works in souls which receive the grace of conversion.[23]

"The forgiveness of sins" is a power of the Church that we confess in the Creed. It is a great power, an awesome authority, and with such power comes great responsibility.

God places a sacred trust in his priests by empowering them to hear our confessions. We place our deepest trust in our priests by confessing our sins to them. The Church guarantees that trust through the *seal of the confessional*.

The seal of the confessional is the priest's duty not to disclose anything he learns from penitents during the Sacrament of Penance. It is absolute and it is sacred. Here is the law laid down by the Church:

> Canon 983: §1. The sacramental seal is inviolable; therefore it is absolutely forbidden for a confessor to betray in any way a penitent in words or in any manner and for any reason.
> §2. The interpreter, if there is one, and all others who in any way have knowledge of sins from confession are also obliged to observe secrecy.

> Canon 984: §1. A confessor is prohibited completely from using knowledge acquired from confession to the detriment of the penitent even when any danger of revelation is excluded.
> §2. A person who has been placed in authority cannot use in any manner for external governance the knowledge about sins which he has received in confession at any time.[24]

If a priest should break the law by any repetition—or even suggestion—of a matter he has learned in the confessional, he incurs automatic excommunication. He is not only suspended from the exercise of his priesthood, but he is forbidden himself to receive any of the sacraments. Only the pope can lift this sentence.

Consider the stark terms in which one priest described his obligation.

So sacredly is confession regarded that if my father had been recently murdered, and you confessed to me that you were the murderer, I would not be allowed to report you; more than that, I would not be permitted to allude to it, nor act differently toward you, if you called at my house immediately after the confession. Information which I receive in the confessional I am not allowed to use or to act on in any way.[25]

It is a trust rarely violated. In matters related to serious crime, a priest may encourage his penitent to surrender to the police, but that is all he can do. A priest cannot himself take action, *in any way*, based on the information he receives in the confessional.

So sacred is this duty that priests have chosen to go to jail rather than testify as a witness against their penitents. In 1813, a magistrate in New York charged a Jesuit priest, Fr. Anthony Kohlmann, with contempt of court for repeatedly refusing to divulge the names of men who had confessed to a particular act of theft. Fr. Kohlmann had persuaded the penitents to make restitution for their crime, and their victim was satisfied with that. But prosecutors held that it was in the public's best interest to put the thieves behind bars.

Fr. Kohlmann would not cooperate, and his case went to the grand jury. It turned on the question of whether a Roman Catholic clergyman could be compelled in any case to disclose the secrets of the confessional. Again and again in cross-examination, he faced interrogation and dire threats, and he answered with silence.

In the end, he was vindicated. In a landmark case regarding religious liberty, the court found Fr. Kohlmann not guilty, and even the Protestant mayor of New York acknowledged, in a public statement, that the seal of the confessional is something essential and sacred to Catholics.[26]

Other priests, in other lands, have not been so fortunate and have been required to serve time in prison or have been executed for their refusal to break the seal. In the fourteenth century, St. John Nepomucene was drowned by order of the king of Bohemia for refusing to divulge secrets of the confessional. More recently, in 1936 during the Spanish Civil War, Fr. Felipe Ciscar Puig was executed for his refusal to reveal what he had heard in the confessional. (He was declared "Blessed" by the Church in 2007.)

In his movie *I Confess*, the director Alfred Hitchcock convincingly depicted a priest who was willing to die rather than expose a murderer who had confessed to him—and then the murderer framed his confessor for the crime! Hitchcock, a Catholic, knew firsthand the power of the seal.

Confession is unique among the sacraments. It is the only one that is administered in secret. The Church observes the other six publicly, with a certain degree of solemnity and with at least a small congregation of witnesses. Penance is the one rite that is all about the penitent—all about you and your relationship with God.

The priest is present as a mediator—as the voice of Christ pronouncing absolution—but that must mark the limit of his involvement with the sins of any penitent. His respect for that limit must be absolute.

The penitent, too, should respect every priest's obligation to keep the seal. If we have confessed certain sins sacramentally, we should not remind Father of them later, when we're outside the confessional. It is good, indeed, to seek additional spiritual direction from a priest, but when we do, we should reintroduce the matter, explaining it from the beginning, as if for the first time.

I find it impossible to overstate the gravity of the seal of the confessional. It is something that every priest senses in a powerful way. We are trained for it. We are ordained for it. We receive it as a grace from God. I know that my brother priests would rather die—and some have died—rather than break this most sacred trust.

From the Pews

Have you ever felt crushed by another person? I have been really hurt by some people in my life, and it would always make me angry and bitter when I thought about what they did. Then I would start to question God. Why did he let this happen? Where was he? Am I a bad person because these things happened to me? I was on this hamster wheel a long time in my life until I found out about the healing power of Confession.

I had confronted the person who had permitted some awful things to happen to me, and that person had basically told me to get over it—it wasn't even a big deal! I took my anger and hatefulness toward this person to Confession. Immediately, the priest set me straight: this person was a child of God too, and I should pray for that person. I was taken aback. Didn't the priest hear what this person had done to me? I left the confessional a little shaken. I was bothered by what the priest said, but slowly I came to realize that I had been set free. I even felt physically healed, like tiny pieces of me were being pulled back together like a puzzle.

This has happened to me repeatedly in Confession, and it is now one of my favorite things to do—really! No matter how ugly and torn up I feel about something, I take it to the Lord, and he takes care of it. Sometimes I don't feel it at that moment in the confessional, but as the week goes on, I can sense being pulled back together and grounded emotionally, spiritually, and even physically.

For instance, just recently, I went to Confession, and the priest went on and on about what seemed to me another topic. However, after some reflection, I realized that what he was saying was perfect for me, and I just had to open my ears to the Holy Spirit talking though the priest.

There are times when I am terrified to go to Confession, and that is when I offer my confession for someone I know who needs prayers. This encourages me to do a complete and thorough confession because I am doing it for someone else.

CHAPTER TEN

THE SACRAMENT OF THE NEW EVANGELIZATION

Y ou know, Father, I should be Catholic. I just sort of drifted away. I miss belonging." The man who offered this self-assessment had just approached me at a charity reception and clearly felt uneasy. We talked for a while, and eventually he admitted, "Even though I was never the best of Catholics, I miss being a part of it all."

Most of us know people like him—people who just drifted away or felt they had a good reason to walk away. Whatever motive they had for leaving, it is time we invited them home.

"They" surround us in great numbers. In many metropolitan areas, the largest religious group is Roman Catholic and the second largest is made up of lapsed Roman Catholics—those who have stopped practicing their faith. Many of them would like to come home; they're just not sure how to do it.

As we grow in our appreciation for the good things of the faith—as we avail ourselves of the banquet of the Eucharist and the luxurious mercy of the confessional—we must not forget those who are, like Lazarus the beggar (Luke 16:19-31), sitting outside in the spiritual cold, far from the doors of the church. Some of them may be materially wealthy, but their souls are impoverished. They need what we have, and perhaps they can't even articulate it. We need to help them.

Think of another image from the Gospels. Remember Jesus' encounter at the pool of Bethesda, by the Sheep Gate in Jerusalem (John 5:2-9). There, we are told, "lay a multitude of invalids, blind, lame, paralyzed" (5:3). They were all waiting for the great "sacramental" moment, the time each day when an angel stirred the waters and someone would be cured. "One man was there who had been ill for thirty-eight years" (5:5). For thirty-eight years he had gone to the pool every day, and yet his turn had never come. Why not?

Jesus asked, "Do you want to be healed?"

The man answered, "Sir, I have no man to put me into the pool when the water is troubled" (John 5:6-7).

What a terrible judgment that man pronounced on Jerusalem! For almost four decades, he had sat within sight of healing. Hundreds and sometimes thousands of people passed him daily. Yet no one would spare the few minutes it would take to help him into the water. Will those passersby face a judgment any different from that of the rich man in Jesus' parable?

We dine at the Lord's sacramental table. We find healing at his font of mercy in the confessional. These are the glad tidings we must announce to the poor in our own day. For there is terrible spiritual poverty in the wealthiest of nations, and if we provide no relief, though we have the means, then we are neglecting our work as Christians. We will be judged for this.

Who are the people in our families, our workplaces, and our neighborhoods who are waiting for us to "give them a lift" and lead them to Confession? Who are the people separated from our table when they should not be?

Remember, the scribes and Pharisees erred not by what they *did*. They practiced the same traditions of piety and offered the same prayers and made the same pilgrimages to Jerusalem as Jesus, Mary, and Joseph. They erred, rather, by what they *didn't* do. They didn't try to reconcile sinners but, instead, left them to die in their sins. They didn't try to bring the family back together; they enjoyed their exclusive place in the company of the religious elite.

We Christians today are no better off if we do not evangelize. "Woe to me," said St. Paul, "if I do not preach the gospel!" (1 Corinthians 9:16), and that should be—it must become—the cry of every Catholic today. Our world needs to hear the message of the prodigal son—the message that all of us, sons and daughters of a prodigal (lavish and generous) Father, can share. If we fail to live by the Sacrament of Confession, and if we fail to share the Good News of the sacrament with others, then we have failed to love.

We have learned great things about the Sacrament of Confession—from the Scriptures, from the lives of the saints, from the stories of modern-day apostles. What will we do with that knowledge?

In 2012 it was my privilege to consider these matters with my brother bishops from around the world. I served as "relator general" when we gathered in Rome for the Synod on the New Evangelization. After many days of discussion, we came to a number of conclusions about effective Christian witness in our time. I'd like to share just one of them with you.

The Sacrament of Penance and Reconciliation is the privileged place to receive God's mercy and forgiveness. It is a place for both personal and communal healing. In this sacrament, all the baptized have a new and personal encounter with Jesus Christ, as well as a new encounter with the Church, facilitating a full reconciliation through the forgiveness of sins. Here the penitent encounters Jesus, and at the same time he or she experiences a deeper appreciation of himself and herself. *The Synod Fathers ask that this sacrament be put again at the center of the pastoral activity of the Church.*

In every diocese, at least one place should be especially dedicated in a permanent way for the celebration of this sacrament, where priests are always present, allowing God's mercy to be experienced by all the faithful. The sacrament should be especially available, even on a daily basis, at places of pilgrimage and specially designated churches. Fidelity to the specific norms which rule the administration of this sacrament is necessary. Every priest should consider the Sacrament of Penance an essential part of his ministry and of the New Evangelization, and in every parish community a suitable time should be set apart for hearing confessions. *(Proposition 33)*

On November 24, 2013, Pope Francis released his first Apostolic Exhortation, *Evangelii Gaudium* [The Joy of the Gospel], which incorporated many elements from the discussions at this Synod. In this document Pope Francis tells us:

Now is the time to say to Jesus: "Lord, I have let myself be deceived; in a thousand ways I have shunned your love, yet here I am once more, to renew my covenant with you. I need you. Save me once again, Lord, take me once more into your redeeming embrace." How good it feels to come back to him whenever we are lost! Let me say this once more: God never tires of forgiving us; we are the ones who tire of seeking his mercy. Christ, who told us to forgive one another "seventy times seven" (Matthew 18:22), has given us his example: he has forgiven us seventy times seven. (*Evangelii Gaudium*, 3)

If we have come to know the joy of the sacrament, we need to share the joy of the sacrament. How could we possibly share the truth of Christianity and yet leave out such Good News about God's mercy? Jesus left us seven sacraments as special channels of his grace, and he designated only two that we may receive frequently.

As Christians, we are compelled to evangelize. One way we keep our faith is to share it. Confession is an important part of that faith—"at the center of the pastoral activity of the Church."

So we shouldn't go alone to Confession when we can share the ride with a friend, a colleague, or a family member—or even more than one other person.

When we invite a friend to Confession, we are not hinting darkly about their personal sinfulness. We should make that very clear. We are simply acknowledging the fallen human condition that we share in common with them and with everyone else. We are testifying to the healing that we ourselves have come to know through reconciliation with God and the Church.

Those who have "drifted away" and "miss being part of it all" need to learn (or re-learn), from you and me, how easy it is to turn and return.

This is our faith. This is the faith of the Church. We profess it in the fourth-century Creed every Sunday when we say that we "believe in . . . the forgiveness of sins." If we believe what we say, we need to proclaim it.

The Sacrament of Reconciliation is the story of God's love that never turns away from us. Aside from the Eucharist, there simply is no greater gift that the Church can give her people. And Confession is our way to a more profound experience of the Eucharist. For those who have been separated from the Church, it is the gateway for their return to the faith and the fold.

Penance is the *sacrament of the New Evangelization*, because it offers us "a new and personal encounter with Jesus Christ, as well as a new encounter with the Church." We can always come home to God, and to the Church, even if we have been away for a long time—and even if we have been there all along but still feel the need to find new life in Christ through this sacramental moment of healing and hope.

From the Pews

One day I was struggling with feelings of guilt over some sins in my life, and a priest I knew was in town for a ministry event. I asked him if he would hear my confession, and he readily agreed. After unfolding for him the mess of my life,

I heard him tell me that I could be a saint one day. I was quite surprised at his insistence and wondered what part of my confession he hadn't heard! After all, I'd just spent the better part of the last ten minutes telling him what a wreck I was. I thought about his words and told him that I wanted to be a saint, to which he started to bounce up and down with utter joy. Over and over again, he said, "It's going to happen!" I got a little excited too and wondered what he knew that I didn't know. He looked at me with such joy and said, "When you want what God wants, it's going to happen!"

My life was changed that day. I began to realize that God wants my sanctity even more than I do, and that reconciliation is a gift from Jesus that aligns my life with the will of God. It is a tangible act that says I want what God wants more than I want to stay in my sin.

Jesus insisted that we forgive one another "seventy times seven," and I have often thought that this was not meant only in our relationships with one another; it was probably the declaration of just how much Christ is willing to always forgive us. Jesus never tires of us coming to him for healing and forgiveness—after all, that is why he gave us the sacrament in the first place. Going to Confession simply means that we are starting to want what God wants for us. We can be the saints he is calling us to be if we begin to cherish and frequent Confession. Thank God for this grace-filled encounter!

THE LORD WAITS FOR US

In a homily at the beginning of his pontificate, Pope Francis observed that sometimes people have difficulty asking for forgiveness. "It is not easy to entrust oneself to God's mercy," he said, "because it is an abyss beyond our comprehension."[27]

But we must do it! We must trust God. We must abandon ourselves to the arms of our Father God.

Pope Francis went on to recall conversations he has had with so many people:

"Oh, Father, if you knew my life, you would not say that to me!"

"Why, what have you done?"

"Oh, I am a great sinner!"

"All the better! Go to Jesus: he likes you to tell him these things!"

He forgets, he has a very special capacity for forgetting. He forgets, he kisses you, he embraces you and he simply says to you: 'Neither do I condemn you; go, and sin no more' (John 8:11). That is the only advice he gives you. After a month, if we are in the same situation . . . let us go back to the Lord. The Lord never tires of forgiving: never! It is we who tire of asking his forgiveness. Let us ask for the grace not to tire of asking forgiveness, because he never tires of forgiving. Let us ask for this grace.

The Lord, who makes all things new, is there, waiting to forgive us, if only we would turn to him and seek his healing love.

Just before he became pope, Cardinal Jorge Bergoglio wrote this in his Lenten message to the people of Buenos Aires:

> Yes, it is possible that everything be made new and different because God continues to be "rich in kindness and mercy, always willing to forgive," and He encourages us to begin again and again. Today we are again invited to undertake a paschal journey to Truth, a journey that includes the cross and renunciation, which will be uncomfortable but not sterile. We are invited to admit that something is not right in ourselves, in society, and in the Church—to change, to turn around, to be converted.[28]

There is still time to return to the Lord. If we have denied him, as St. Peter did, let us seek his forgiveness. If we have betrayed him, as Judas did, let us repent and be reconciled by seeking his pardon. Our sins, though they be like scarlet, shall be made white as snow by God's love (Isaiah 1:18). The Lord never hesitates or tires of forgiving, so let us never hesitate or tire of asking—with confidence, with trust—for forgiveness.

From the Pews

"Bless me father for I have sinned. It has been thirteen years since my last confession."

And what a thirteen years it had been! While most of my friends were enjoying the freedom of college, I got married and had a baby. But I still had the youthful urges of my peers. I was rebellious. I wanted to experiment. And I did not want to mindlessly follow the same religious path of my parents; I wanted to forge my own, so I went to different churches—but only when I felt like it. Even though I was a young mother, I fell into a hedonistic lifestyle. Parties, happy hours, experimentation with alcohol and drugs—St. Augustine had nothing on me!

Eventually, I realized that my freewheeling life was not very healthy or fulfilling, and it was a terrible example for our growing daughter. By the grace of God, I was led to reexamine my life and my faith through a group for lapsed Catholics. Earlier, I had been feeling so empty, but now, to my amazement, the Mass was suddenly coming alive for me! After much soul-searching, I decided to return to my Catholic faith. But I still had some anxiety about making my first confession after thirteen years of living in the fast lane.

On the day that I finally got the courage to go to Confession, I just unloaded my soul to the priest. I figured if his afternoon had been routine, my guilty admissions would surely liven up his day! But he was welcoming, compassionate, and very patient with me. After I was done, I felt like a huge burden had just been lifted from my shoulders, not to mention my very soul. I was thoroughly cleansed and could start a new life.

That is the beauty of Confession. From that day on, with the reinforcement of regular trips to the confessional, I embarked on a new spiritual path, and I've never looked back.

RITE FOR THE RECONCILIATION OF INDIVIDUAL PENITENTS

Reception of the Penitent and Invitation to Trust in God

When the penitent comes to confess his sins, the priest welcomes him warmly and greets him with kindness.

Then the penitent makes the Sign of the Cross, which the priest may make also.

In the name of the Father,
and of the Son,
and of the Holy Spirit. Amen.

The priest invites the penitent to have trust in God, in these or similar words:

May God, who has enlightened every heart,
help you to know your sins
and trust in his mercy.

The penitent answers: Amen.

Other forms of reception of the penitent may be chosen.

Reading of the Word of God (Optional)

Then the priest may read or say from memory a text of Scripture which proclaims God's mercy and calls man to conversion.

A reading may also be chosen from those given for the reconciliation of several penitents. The priest and penitent may choose other readings from Scripture.

(Sample:) 1 John 1:6-7, 9

> If we say, "We have fellowship with him," while we continue to walk in darkness, we lie and do not act in truth. But if we walk in the light as he is in the light, then we have fellowship with one another, and the blood of his Son Jesus cleanses us from all sin. If we acknowledge our sins, he is faithful and just and will forgive our sins and cleanse us from every wrongdoing. (NAB)

Other readings

Confession of Sins and Acceptance of Satisfaction

Where it is the custom, the penitent says a general formula for confession (for example, I confess to almighty God) before he/she confesses his/her sins.

If necessary, the priest helps the penitent to make an integral confession and gives him suitable counsel. He urges him to be sorry for his faults, reminding him that through the Sacrament of Penance the Christian dies and rises with Christ and is thus renewed in the paschal mystery. The priest proposes an act of penance, which the penitent accepts to make satisfaction for sin and to amend his life.

The priest should make sure that he adapts his counsel to the penitent's circumstances.

Prayer of the Penitent and Absolution

The priest then asks the penitent to express his sorrow, which the penitent may do in these or similar words:

My God,
I am sorry for my sins with all my heart.
In choosing to do wrong
and failing to do good,
I have sinned against you
whom I should love above all things.
I firmly intend, with your help,
to do penance,
to sin no more,
and to avoid whatever leads me to sin.
Our Savior Jesus Christ
suffered and died for us.
In his name, my God, have mercy.

Or:

Lord Jesus, Son of God,
have mercy on me, a sinner.

Other prayers of the penitent may be chosen.

A b s o l u t i o n

Then the priest extends his hands over the penitent's head (or at least extends his right hand) and says:

God, the Father of mercies,
through the death and resurrection of his Son
has reconciled the world to himself
and sent the Holy Spirit among us
for the forgiveness of sins;
through the ministry of the Church
may God give you pardon and peace,
**and I absolve you from your sins
in the name of the Father, and of the Son,
and of the Holy Spirit.**

The penitent answers: Amen.

After the absolution, the priest continues:

Give thanks to the Lord, for he is good.

The penitent concludes:

His mercy endures for ever.

Then the priest dismisses the penitent who has been reconciled, saying:

The Lord has freed you from your sins. Go in peace.

Or:

May the Passion of our Lord Jesus Christ,
the intercession of the Blessed Virgin and of all the saints,
whatever good you do and suffering you endure,
heal your sins,
help you to grow in holiness,
and reward you with eternal life.
Go in peace.

Or:

The Lord has freed you from sin.
May he bring you safely to his kingdom in heaven.
Glory to him for ever.

Or:

Blessed are those
whose sins have been forgiven,
whose evil deeds have been forgotten.
Rejoice in the Lord,
and go in peace.

Or:

Go in peace,
and proclaim to the world
the wonderful works of God,
who has brought you salvation.

HELPFUL PRAYERS

Prayer to the Holy Spirit

(To begin an examination of conscience)

Come Holy Spirit, fill the hearts of your faithful
and kindle in them the fire of your love.
V. Send forth your Spirit, and they shall be created.
R. And You shall renew the face of the earth.
Let us pray.
O God, who by the light of the Holy Spirit,
did instruct the hearts of the faithful,
grant that by the same Holy Spirit,
we may be truly wise and ever enjoy his consolations,
through Christ Our Lord. Amen.

Act of Contrition

O my God, I am heartily sorry for having offended you, and
I detest all my sins, because of your just punishments; but
most of all because they offend you, my God, who are all
good and deserving of all my love. I firmly resolve, with the
help of your grace, to confess my sins, to do penance, and to
amend my life. Amen.

APPENDIX C

A BRIEF EXAMINATION OF CONSCIENCE

This is the examination distributed as part of "The Light Is ON for You" program. It is based on the Ten Commandments and the Two Great Commandments of Jesus.

The Ten Commandments

I am the Lord your God: you shall not have strange gods before me.

Have I treated people, events, or things as more important than God?

You shall not take the name of the Lord your God in vain.

Have my words, actively or passively, put down God, the Church, or people?

Remember to keep holy the Lord's Day.

Do I go to Mass every Sunday (or Saturday Vigil) and on Holy Days of Obligation (January 1; the Ascension; August 15; November 1; December 8; December 25)? Do I avoid, when possible, work that impedes worship to God, joy for the Lord's Day, and proper relaxation of mind and body?

Do I look for ways to spend time with family or in service on Sunday?

Honor your father and your mother.

Do I show my parents due respect? Do I seek to maintain good communication with my parents where possible? Do I criticize them for lacking skills I think they should have?

You shall not kill.

Have I harmed another through physical, verbal, or emotional means, including gossip or manipulation of any kind?

You shall not commit adultery.

Have I respected the physical and sexual dignity of others and of myself?

You shall not steal.

Have I taken or wasted time or resources that belonged to another?

You shall not bear false witness against your neighbor.

Have I gossiped, told lies, or embellished stories at the expense of another?

You shall not covet your neighbor's spouse.

Have I honored my spouse with my full affection and exclusive love?

You shall not covet your neighbor's goods.

Am I content with my own means and needs, or do I compare myself to others unnecessarily?

Christ's Two Commandments

How well do we love God and others? Do we love as Christ calls us to? In the Gospel of Matthew, Christ gives us two Commandments: "He said to him, 'You shall love the Lord, your God, with all your heart, with all your soul and with all your mind. This is the greatest and the first commandment. The second is like it: You shall love your neighbor as yourself. The whole law and the prophets depend on these two commandments'" (Matthew 22:37-40, NAB).

Not sure what love is? St. Paul describes it for us in his Letter to the Corinthians. Is this how you love God and others? "Love is patient, love is kind. It is not jealous, [love] is not pompous, it is not inflated, it is not rude, it does not seek its own interests, it is not quick-tempered, it does not brood over injury, it does not rejoice over wrongdoing but rejoices with the truth. It bears all things, believes all things, hopes all things, endures all things. Love never fails" (1 Corinthians 13:4-8, NAB).

A Longer Examination of Conscience

Especially for someone who has been away from the sacrament for a long time, a longer examination of conscience is a good way to prepare for Confession. The U.S. bishops have prepared specialized examinations of conscience for Catholics in different states of life and at different stages of life: children, young adults, single people, and married people.[29] There is also a special examination based on Catholic social teaching. These are included here.

Routine daily examinations of conscience, however, need not be so extensive. For those who confess their sins with some regularity, it could be enough to recall the day's events while reflecting upon a simple list of the Ten Commandments or the Beatitudes.

An Examination of Conscience for Married Persons

Responsibilities to God:

- Have I gone to Mass every Sunday? Have I participated at Mass or have I daydreamed or been present with a blank mind?
- Have I prayed every day (15–20 minutes)?
- Have I read the Bible? Have I studied the truths of our

faith and allowed them to become more part of the way I think and act? Have I read any spiritual books or religious literature?

- Have I told God that I want to love him with my whole heart, mind, and strength? Do I hold any resentments toward God?
- Have I recognized my need for Jesus and his salvation? Have I asked the Holy Spirit to empower me to live the Christian life, to be a proper husband/wife and parent?
- Have I been financially generous to the Church? Have I participated in parish or religious activities?
- Have I held resentments toward the Church or Church authorities? Have I forgiven them?

Responsibilities to my spouse:

- Have I cared for my spouse? Have I been generous with my time? Have I been affectionate and loving? Have I told my spouse that I love him or her?
- Have I been concerned about the spiritual well-being of my spouse?
- Have I listened to my spouse? Have I paid attention to his other concerns, worries, and problems? Have I sought these out?
- Have I allowed resentments and bitterness toward my spouse to take root in my mind? Have I nurtured these? Have I forgiven my spouse for the wrongs he or she has committed against me?
- Have I allowed misunderstanding, miscommunication or

accidents to cause anger and mistrust? Have I nurtured critical and negative thoughts about my spouse?

- Have I manipulated my spouse in order to get my own way?
- Have I tried to bully or overpower my spouse?
- Have I spoken sharply or sarcastically to my spouse? Have I spoken in a demeaning or negative way? Have I injured my spouse through taunting and negative teasing? Have I called my spouse harsh names or used language that is not respectful?
- Have I physically abused my spouse?
- Have I gossiped about my spouse?
- Have I undermined the authority and dignity of my spouse through disrespect and rebelliousness?
- Have I been moody and sullen?
- Have I bickered with my spouse out of stubbornness and selfishness?
- Have I lied or been deceitful to my spouse?
- Have I misused sexuality? Have I used sexual relations solely for my own selfish pleasure? Have I been too demanding in my desire for sexual fulfillment? Have I been loving and physically affectionate in my sexual relations or have I used sexual relations in a way that would be demeaning or disrespectful to my spouse? Have I refused sexual relations out of laziness, revenge, or manipulation?
- Have I refused to conceive children out of selfishness or material greed? Have I used artificial means of contraception?
- Have I had an abortion or encouraged others to have one?

- Have I masturbated?
- Have I flirted or fostered improper relationships with someone else, either in my mind or through words and actions?
- Have I used pornography: books, magazines, or movies?
- Have I committed adultery?
- Have I misused alcohol or drugs?
- Have I been financially responsible?

Responsibilities to children:

- Have I cared for the spiritual needs of my children? Have I been a shepherd and guardian as God has appointed me? Have I tried to foster a Christian family where Jesus is Lord? Have I taught my children the gospel and the commandments of God?
- Have I prayed with them?
- Have I been persistent and courageous in my training and teaching? Have I disciplined them when necessary? Have I been lazy and apathetic?
- Have I talked with them to find out their problems, concerns, and fears? Have I been affectionate toward them? Have I hugged them and told them that I love them? Have I played or recreated with them?
- Have I been impatient and frustrated with them? Have I corrected them out of love in order to teach them what is right and good? Have I treated them with respect? Have I spoken to them in a sarcastic or demeaning way?
- Have I held resentments against them? Have I forgiven them?

- Have I been of one heart and mind with my spouse in the upbringing of the children? Or have I allowed disagreements and dissension to disrupt the training, educating, and disciplining of our children?
- Have I undermined the role of authority in the eyes of my children by speaking negatively against God, the Church, my spouse, or others who hold legitimate authority over them?
- Have I been a good Christian witness to my children in what I say and do? Or do I demand one standard for them and another for myself?
- Have I been properly generous with my children regarding money and physical and material well-being? Have I been miserly? Have I been extravagant, thus spoiling them?

Responsibilities to society:

- Have I been a Christian witness to those with whom I work or associate? Have I spoken to anyone about the gospel and how important it is to believe in Jesus?
- Have I held resentments and anger against those with whom I work, relatives, or friends? Have I forgiven them?
- Have I been unethical in my business dealings? Have I stolen or lied?
- Have I allowed the gospel to influence my political and social opinions?
- Have I had a proper Christian concern for the poor and needy?
- Have I paid my taxes?

- Have I fostered or nurtured hatred toward my "political" enemies, either local, national, or international?
- Have I been prejudiced toward others because of race, color, religion, or social status?

An Examination of Conscience for Single Persons

Responsibilities to God:

- Have I gone to Mass every Sunday? Have I participated at Mass or have I daydreamed or been present with a blank mind?
- Have I prayed every day (15–20 minutes)?
- Have I read the Bible? Have I studied the truths of our faith and allowed them to become more a part of the way I think and act? Have I read any spiritual books or religious literature?
- Have I told God that I want to love him with my whole heart, mind, and strength? Do I hold any resentments toward God?
- Have I recognized my need for Jesus and his salvation? Have I asked the Holy Spirit to empower me to live the Christian life?
- Have I been financially generous to the Church? Have I participated in parish or religious activities?
- Have I held resentments toward the Church or Church authorities? Have I forgiven them?

Responsibilities to others and to myself:

- Have I been rebellious, disobedient, or disrespectful to anyone in authority?
- Have I lied to or deceived others—friends, boss, or co-workers?
- Have I been arrogant and stubborn?
- Have I gotten angry or nurtured and held grudges and resentments?
- Have I refused to forgive others—parents, relatives, employers, a former friend, a former spouse? Have I cultivated hatred?
- Have I felt sorry for myself or nurtured self-pity?
- Have I engaged in sexual fantasies? Have I looked at others lustfully?
- Have I read pornographic literature or looked at pornographic pictures, shows, or movies?
- Have I masturbated?
- Have I lustfully kissed or sexually touched someone? Have I had sexual intercourse? Have I had an abortion or encouraged another to have one?
- Have I gossiped about others? Have I slandered anyone? Have I told lies about others? Have I mocked or made fun of others?

Responsibilities to society:

• Have I been a Christian witness to those with whom I work or associate? Have I spoken to anyone about the gospel and how important it is to believe in Jesus?
• Have I allowed the gospel to influence my political and social opinions?
• Have I had a proper Christian concern for the poor and needy?
• Have I paid my taxes?
• Have I fostered or nurtured hatred toward my "political" opponents, either local, national, or international?
• Have I been prejudiced toward others because of race, color, religion, or social status?

An Examination of Conscience for Young Adults

Responsibilities to God:

• Have I gone to Mass on Sunday or have I rebelled and been stubborn about going to Mass?
• Did I participate in the Mass, or did I daydream?
• Have I prayed every day?
• Have I read the Bible?
• Have I been rebellious toward God and his commands?
• Have I misused the name of God by swearing and cursing?
• Have I told the Father that I love him for creating me and making me his son/daughter?

- Have I thanked Jesus for becoming man, dying for my sin, and rising to give me eternal life?
- Have I asked the Holy Spirit to help me conquer sin and temptation and to be obedient to God's commands?

Responsibilities to others and myself:

- Have I been rebellious, disobedient, or disrespectful to my parents, teachers, and those in authority over me?
- Have I lied to or deceived my parents or others?
- Have I been arrogant and stubborn?
- Have I talked back to my parents or those in authority?
- Have I gotten angry or nurtured and held grudges and resentments? Have I refused to forgive others? Have I cultivated hatred?
- Have I engaged in sexual fantasies? Have I looked at others lustfully?
- Have I read pornographic literature or looked at pornographic pictures, shows, or movies?
- Have I masturbated?
- Have I lustfully kissed or sexually touched someone? Have I had sexual intercourse?
- Have I had an abortion or encouraged another to have one?
- Have I gossiped about others? Have I slandered anyone? Have I told lies about others? Have I mocked or made fun of others?
- Have I lied or cheated? Have I stolen anything? Have I paid it back?

- Have I been selfish or spiteful toward others? Have I been jealous?
- Have I gotten drunk or taken drugs?
- Have I participated in anything that is of the occult: ouija boards, fortune-tellers, séances, channeling, astrology?
- Have I been patient, kind, gentle, and self-controlled?
- When my conscience told me to do something good, did I do it or did I ignore it?

An Examination of Conscience for Children

Responsibilities to God:

- Have I prayed every day?
- Have I prayed my morning prayers and night prayers?
- Have I prayed with my parents and family?
- Have I been moody and rebellious about praying and going to church on Sunday?
- Have I asked the Holy Spirit to help me whenever I have been tempted to sin?
- Have I asked the Holy Spirit to help me do what is right?

Responsibilities to others:

- Have I been obedient and respectful to my parents?
- Have I lied or been deceitful to them or to others?
- Have I been arrogant, stubborn, or rebellious?
- Have I talked back to parents, teachers, or other adults?

- Have I pouted and been moody?
- Have I been selfish toward my parents, brothers and sisters, teachers, or my friends and schoolmates?
- Have I gotten angry at them? Have I hit anyone?
- Have I held grudges or not forgiven others?
- Have I treated other children with respect or have I made fun of them and called them names?
- Have I used bad language?
- Have I stolen anything? Have I returned it?
- Have I performed my responsibilities, such as homework and household chores?
- Have I been helpful and affectionate toward my family?
- Have I been kind and generous with my friends?

Examination of Conscience Based on Catholic Social Teaching

Life and Dignity of the Human Person:

- Do I respect the life and dignity of every human person from conception through natural death?
- Do I recognize the face of Christ reflected in all others around me whatever their race, class, age, or abilities?
- Do I work to protect the dignity of others when it is being threatened?
- Am I committed to both protecting human life and to ensuring that every human being is able to live in dignity?

Call to Family, Community, and Participation:

- Do I try to make positive contributions in my family and in my community?
- Are my beliefs, attitudes, and choices such that they strengthen or undermine the institution of the family?
- Am I aware of problems facing my local community and involved in efforts to find solutions? Do I stay informed and make my voice heard when needed?
- Do I support the efforts of poor persons to work for change in their neighborhoods and communities? Do my attitudes and interactions empower or disempower others?

Rights and Responsibilities:

- Do I recognize and respect the economic, social, political, and cultural rights of others?
- Do I live in material comfort and excess while remaining insensitive to the needs of others whose rights are unfulfilled?
- Do I take seriously my responsibility to ensure that the rights of persons in need are realized?
- Do I urge those in power to implement programs and policies that give priority to human dignity and the rights of all, especially the vulnerable?

Option for the Poor and Vulnerable:

- Do I give special attention to the needs of the poor and vulnerable in my community and in the world?
- Am I disproportionately concerned for my own good at the expense of others?
- Do I engage in service and advocacy work that protects the dignity of poor and vulnerable persons?

The Dignity of Work and the Rights of Workers:

- As a worker, do I give my employer a fair day's work for my wages? As an owner, do I treat workers fairly?
- Do I treat all workers with whom I interact with respect, no matter their position or class?
- Do I support the rights of all workers to adequate wages, health insurance, vacation, and sick leave? Do I affirm their right to form or join unions or worker associations?
- Do my purchasing choices take into account the hands involved in the production of what I buy? When possible, do I buy products produced by workers whose rights and dignity were respected?

Solidarity:

- Does the way I spend my time reflect a genuine concern for others?
- Is solidarity incorporated into my prayer and spirituality?
-

Do I lift up vulnerable people throughout the world in my prayer, or is it reserved for only my personal concerns?

- Am I attentive only to my local neighbors or also those across the globe?
- Do I see all members of the human family as my brothers and sisters?

Care for God's Creation:

- Do I live out my responsibility to care for God's creation?
- Do I see my care for creation as connected to my concern for poor persons, who are most at risk from environmental problems?
- Do I litter? Live wastefully? Use energy too freely? Are there ways I could reduce consumption in my life?
- Are there ways I could change my daily practices and those of my family, school, workplace, or community to better conserve the earth's resources for future generations?

A Brief Glossary of Terms Related to Confession

Most definitions are adapted from the glossary in the English edition of the Catechism of the Catholic Church.

Absolution: An essential element of the Sacrament of Penance in which the priest, by the power entrusted to the Church by Christ, pardons the sin(s) of the penitent.

Binding and Loosing: The disciplinary authority Jesus gave to his apostles; their power to forgive sins or retain them.

Confession: An essential element of the Sacrament of Penance and Reconciliation, which consists in telling one's sins to the priestly minister. By extension, the word "confession" is used to refer to the Sacrament of Penance itself.

Contrition: Sorrow of the soul and hatred for the sin committed, together with a resolution not to sin again. Contrition is the most important act of the penitent, and is necessary for the reception of the Sacrament of Penance.

Examination of Conscience: Prayerful self-reflection on our words and deeds in the light of the gospel to determine how we may have sinned against God. The reception of the

Sacrament of Penance ought to be prepared for by such an examination of conscience.

General Confession: A private confession in which the penitent resolves to confess as far as possible all past sins.

Liturgy: The ritual public worship of the Church. Through the liturgy, Christ, our high priest, continues the work of our redemption through the Church's celebration of the paschal mystery by which he accomplished our salvation.

Mortal Sin: A grave infraction of the law of God that destroys the divine life in the soul of the sinner (sanctifying grace), constituting a turn away from God. For a sin to be mortal, three conditions must be present: grave matter, full knowledge of the evil of the act, and full consent of the will.

Penance: *Interior* penance is a conversion of heart toward God and away from sin, which implies the intention to change one's life because of hope in divine mercy. *External* acts of penance include fasting, prayer, and almsgiving. In sacramental Confession, the priest usually assigns some act of penance for the penitent to perform.

Penitent: The sinner who repents of sin and seeks forgiveness.

Reconciliation: The sacramental celebration in which, through God's mercy and forgiveness, the sinner is reconciled with God and also with the Church, Christ's body, which is wounded by sin.

Sacrament: An efficacious sign of grace, instituted by Christ and entrusted to the Church, by which divine life is dispensed to us through the work of the Holy Spirit. The sacraments (called "mysteries" in the Eastern Churches) are seven in number: Baptism, Confirmation, Eucharist, Penance or Reconciliation, Anointing of the Sick, Holy Orders, and Matrimony.

Satisfaction: An act whereby the sinner makes amends for sin, especially in reparation to God for offenses against him. The penance given by the confessor in the Sacrament of Penance constitutes such satisfaction. All true satisfaction for sin must be a participation in the satisfaction for sin made by Christ through his death on the cross.

Seal of the Confessional: The confessor's obligation to keep absolutely secret what a penitent has told to him in the Sacrament of Penance; also known as the "sacramental seal."

Sin: An offense against God as well as a fault against reason, truth, and right conscience. Sin is a deliberate thought, word, deed, or omission contrary to the eternal law of God. In judging the gravity of sin, it is customary to distinguish between mortal and venial sins

Venial Sin: Sin that does not destroy the divine life in the soul, as does mortal sin, though it diminishes and wounds it. Venial sin is the failure to observe necessary moderation, in lesser matters of the moral law, or in grave matters acting without full knowledge or complete consent.

Endnotes

1. Tertullian, *On Penance* 12.

2. Jerome, *Commentariorum In Sophoniam Prophetam* 1.10

3. Nathaniel Hawthorne, *The Marble Faun: The Romance of Monte Beni* (Boston: Houghton, Mifflin, 1883), 405.

4. Charlotte Bronte, *Villette* (London: John Murray, 1932), 89.

5. April Oursler Armstrong, *The House with a Hundred Gates: A Memoir* (New York: McGraw-Hill, 1965), 162–63.

6. St. Augustine of Hippo, Sermon 392.

7. Pope Francis, General Audience, November 20, 2013.

8. Mother Teresa, *No Greater Love* (Novato, CA: New World Library, 1989), 112.

9. William Blake, "A Poison Tree," from *Songs of Experience*, 1794.

10. Dion DiMucci tells his story in the memoir *Dion: The Wanderer Talks Truth* (Ann Arbor, MI: Servant, 2011).

11. Letter from George Bernard Shaw to G. K. Chesterton, February 16, 1923, cited in *Gilbert Keith Chesterton*, by Maise Ward.

12. C.K. Chesterton, *Autobiography of C. K. Chesterton*, San Francisco: Ignatius Press, 2006, 324–25.

13. Based on an interview with the French magazine *Paris-Match*.

14. Madame de Barberey, *Elizabeth Seton* (Emmitsburg, MD: Mother Seton Guild Press, 1957), 142.

15. Ladislaus Kluz, *Kolbe and the Commandant* (Chicago: DeSmet, 1983), 267.

16. Kurt Klinger, *A Pope Laughs: Stories of John XXIII* (New York: Holt, Rinehart, and Winston, 1964), 51.

17. Pope John XXIII, *Journal of a Soul* (New York: Signet, 1965), 68.

18. Ibid.

19. Archbishop Anthony Bloom, *Beginning to Pray* (Mahwah, NJ: Paulist, 1970), 27.

20. Pope John XXIII, *Journal of a Soul*, 82.

21. Pope Pius XII, radio message to the United States Catechetical Congress in Boston, October 26, 1946.

22. Pope John Paul II, Apostolic Exhortation *Reconciliation and Penance*, 1984.

23. John Paul II, *Gift and Mystery: On the Fiftieth Anniversary of My Priestly Ordination* (New York: Doubleday, 1996), 86.

24. The Code of Canon Law can be accessed on the Vatican website, www.vatican.va.

25. Bishop John Francis Noll, *Father Smith Instructs Jackson* (Huntington, IN: Our Sunday Visitor, 1951), 171.

26. For details of the Kohlmann case, see the excellent account of historian James Garrity, "Religious Freedom at Heart of New York Case Two Centuries Ago," published in *Catholic New York*, June 27, 2012, and available on the website cny.org.

27. Pope Francis, Homily, March 17, 2013.

28. "Cardinal Bergoglio's Lenten Message for Buenos Aires," Zenit News Service, March 14, 2013, Zenit.org, http://www.zenit.org/en/articles/cardinal-bergoglio-s-lenten-message-for-buenos-aires.

29. These examinations can be accessed at the U.S. Conference of Catholic Bishops website at http://www.usccb.org/prayer-and-worship/sacraments/penance/examinations-of-conscience.cfm. All but the examination based on Catholic social teaching are authored by Fr. Thomas Weinandy and are reprinted with permission of the author.

**His Eminence Cardinal Donald Wuerl** is the Archbishop of Washington and was elevated to the College of Cardinals in 2010 by Pope Benedict XVI. Known for his efforts on behalf of Catholic education, he has served as chairman of the United States Conference of Catholic Bishops' Committee on Doctrine, Committee on Education, Committee on Priestly Life and Ministry, and Committee on Priestly Formation, and is a member of the USCCB Committee on Evangelization. He also served as the Relator General for the Vatican Synod of Bishops on the New Evangelization for the Transmission of the Christian Faith. He is the author of numerous articles and books, including *Faith That Transforms Us: Reflections on the Creed* (The Word Among Us Press, 2013).

The Cardinal was born in Pittsburgh, Pennsylvania, and received graduate degrees from the Catholic University of America, the Gregorian University while attending the North American College, and a doctorate in theology from the University of Saint Thomas in Rome. He was ordained to the priesthood on December 17, 1966, and was ordained a bishop by Pope John Paul II on January 6, 1986, in St. Peter's Basilica. He served as auxiliary bishop in Seattle until 1987 and then as bishop of Pittsburgh for eighteen years until his appointment to Washington. His titular church in Rome is Saint Peter in Chains.

the WORD among us ®
The *Spirit* of Catholic Living

This book was published by The Word Among Us. Since 1981, The Word Among Us has been answering the call of the Second Vatican Council to help Catholic laypeople encounter Christ in the Scriptures.

The name of our company comes from the prologue to the Gospel of John and reflects the vision and purpose of all of our publications: to be an instrument of the Spirit, whose desire is to manifest Jesus' presence in and to the children of God. In this way, we hope to contribute to the Church's ongoing mission of proclaiming the gospel to the world so that all people would know the love and mercy of our Lord and grow ever more deeply in love with him.

Our monthly devotional magazine, *The Word Among Us*, features meditations on the daily and Sunday Mass readings, and currently reaches more than one million Catholics in North America and another half million Catholics in one hundred countries around the world. Our book division, The Word Among Us Press, publishes numerous books, Bible studies, and pamphlets that help Catholics grow in their faith.

To learn more about who we are and what we publish, log on to our website at www.wau.org. There you will find a variety of Catholic resources that will help you grow in your faith.

Embrace His Word, Listen to God . . .

www.wau.org